PREFIX	NUMBER	PRICE
LABEL		DISTRIBUTOR
ARTIST		
TITLE		
DATE:		ORDER

Orson Welles

ORSON WELLES

a celebration by John Russell Taylor

Picture research by The Kobal Collection

PAVILION
MICHAEL JOSEPH

First published in Great Britain 1986 by
Pavilion Books Limited
196 Shaftesbury Avenue, London WC2H 8JL
in association with Michael Joseph Limited
27 Wrights Lane, Kensington, London W8 5TZ

British Library Cataloguing in Publication Data

Taylor, John Russell
    Orson Welles: a celebration.
    1. Welles, Orson   2. Moving-picture
    producers and directors—United States
    —Biography
    I. Title
    791.43′0233′0924   PN1998.A3.W/

ISBN 1–85145–002–5

Designed by Lawrence Edwards

Filmset and printed in Great Britain
by BAS Printers Limited
Bound by Hunter & Foulis Limited

CONTENTS

INTRODUCTION

RIGHT AT THE END OF CITIZEN KANE, THERE IS A wonderful image which conveys something of the magnitude and the mystery of the just-dead Kane by means of a bewildering array of boxes and cases and trunks, most of them unopened, in which the disregarded by-products of a lifetime's amassing have been left to challenge the speculation of generations to come. Orson Welles's own life, looked at in the perspective created by his death at the age of seventy, seems very like that, and the temptation to see *Citizen Kane*, the masterpiece he created at the age of twenty-five, as an almost uncanny prefiguration of his own development, or possibly as the film he chose (unconsciously) to make himself into, is irresistible.

Should we, like the almost faceless reporter in *Citizen Kane*, set out to rifle yet again through the confused and conflicting information on his life and personality, the films he did, and didn't, and didn't quite make, in order to find his own personal 'Rosebud', that one piece of evidence with which all the other pieces will fall neatly into place? Or are we starting the wrong way round, still following Welles's own misleading directions even after he is no longer there to pronounce them? Perhaps the truth is rather that his tragedy was to find his Rosebud too soon, and ever afterwards to go on wondering what happened next. Or, as one director of his play *Moby Dick – Rehearsed* put it, that Orson Welles was Ahab – the only difference was that he caught his white whale right at the start, and spent the rest of his life looking for another.

Undeniably, Welles was and is a mystery – it is appropriate enough that his favourite image for the artist in general and himself in particular was that of a stage magician, an illusionist whose stock-in-trade is to wrap the perfectly explicable and often very simple (once you know the trick) in a cloak of obscurity and mystification. If you asked the real Orson Welles to stand up and be recognized, a dozen different people would immediately spring to their feet, claiming to be the man. Did he do

this deliberately? Perhaps yes, perhaps no – perhaps a bit of each. Consider, for example, the long trail of unrealized projects and unfinished works which ran through his life right from *The Magnificent Ambersons* in 1942 to his death, when he was supposedly just about to start work on yet another new film (or three, or five). Among the abandoned were, at least, *It's All True*, his government-encouraged Pan-American extravaganza, *Moby Dick* (based on his London stage production), *Don Quixote*, *The Deep* (alias *Dead Reckoning* alias *Dead Calm*) and *The Other Side of the Wind*. Was Charles Higham (and many after him) right to blame much of this on a neurotic fear of completion, a deep-seated conviction that anything he might show the world would inevitably be compared with *Citizen Kane* and found wanting? Welles's most authorized biographer pooh-poohs this theory – why, she asks, would he spend so much time, and so much of his own money, on these projects if he did not seriously mean to complete them? And certainly, film by film, the explanations Welles offered for non-completion (mostly financial) sound reasonable enough. But taking them in the aggregate, one begins to wonder. Even Welles began to wonder, seeing himself as a man who, every time he steps out of doors, gets struck by lightning. As well ask why, if he sincerely wanted to be thin, he allowed himself to get so fat that, towards the end, he could hardly move unaided. When we come to the realm of unconscious motivation, one man's hypothesis is as good as another's.

Maybe Welles answered the question, or maybe he ducked out of it altogether (it's hard to be sure), with the story he told in the character of the mysterious Mr Arkadin in *Confidential Report*. A scorpion asked a frog to give him a ride across a river on his back. The frog was dubious. 'But what if you sting me?' he said. 'Why should I sting you?' said the scorpion; 'I couldn't do that without destroying myself as well.' Persuaded, the frog set out

across the river with the scorpion on his back; and halfway across, the scorpion stung him anyway. As they both sank, the frog protested, 'There is no logic in this.' To which the drowning scorpion replied, 'I know . . . it's my character.' Undoubtedly many of Welles's failures and disasters derived from this character, in all its grandeur and perversity. But then again, some of them just happened: people do, after all, occasionally get struck by lighting – even Orson Welles. Or stung by scorpions for no logical reason. Looking back now on his life, one cannot but ask: which was he more, the scorpion or the frog?

John Russell Taylor

Growing up
to be a
genius

1

GEORGE ORSON WELLES WAS BORN IN KENOSHA, Wisconsin, on 6 May 1915. That much, through the tangle of legend woven around his early life by Welles himself, seems to be clear. He was the second son of Richard Head Welles, an inventor, and his wife Beatrice Ives, a concert pianist. At least, that is how Orson (the George was soon dropped as unbecomingly plebian) used to describe them, and it is close enough to the truth. His father was a sporty type who had made a reasonable amount of money (not rich compared with J. Pierpont Morgan, but more than comfortable) manufacturing bicycle and car lamps of a carbide-powered kind he had invented, selling his business shrewdly when they were about to be universally replaced with electric lamps. He continued to dabble with invention during Welles's early childhood, though never again with any recorded success. His mother was the child of a once-rich family, now in relatively reduced circumstances. She had been brought up to revere artistic achievement, and was no mean pianist herself, though she began to play professionally only after her marriage broke up when Welles himself was six.

And then there was the third parent – for how could one expect anyone as extraordinary as Welles to make do with the regulation two? This was the local doctor, a Russian-Jewish orthopedist called Maurice Bernstein who was (in a strictly platonic way, we are told) a passionate admirer of Mrs Welles, and allegedly, on first catching sight of the infant Orson, aged eighteen months, declared him to be without doubt a genius. From then on Dr Bernstein became a fixture in the household, his (strictly platonic) obsession with the child equalling if not surpassing his obsession with the mother. He showered Orson with significant gifts (paints, a violin, a puppet theatre, a magic kit), and virtually took over the direction of Orson's life, to such an extent that Orson called him 'Dadda' (his own father's reactions being unrecorded but presumably dubious) and the good doctor called him 'Pookles'. A

further excuse for his constant attendance was provided by the general sickliness of Beatrice and the extraordinary catalogue of illnesses Orson went through as a child.

When Orson was four his father moved the family to Chicago, perhaps in hopes of escaping Dr Bernstein's attentions – but if so the idea was frustrated when Bernstein almost immediately followed them. Through Bernstein, who was always pressing the all-purpose juvenile prodigy to perform, and through his mother's genuine musical talents, the young Welles rapidly came into contact with Chicago musical society, and took his first, already confident, steps on stage with, initially, a walk-on in the Chicago Opera's production of *Samson and Delilah* (can that be why the hapless Susan Alexander's disastrous Chicago operatic début in *Citizen Kane* is in close imitation of *Samson and Delilah*?) and then in the more important – though of course non-singing role of Butterfly's love-child Trouble in *Madame Butterfly*. He also got a temporary job dressed up as a rabbit at Marshall Fields, directing customers to the woollen underwear on the eighth floor.

Shortly after Welles's sixth birthday the strains of his parents' marriage became unbearable, and they formally separated, his father taking off and his mother remaining to pursue her musical ambitions (with some success) in Chicago.

Welles lived most of the time with his mother – and 'Dadda' Bernstein, of course – but used quite regularly to holiday and travel with his father. He later claimed to have been conceived in Rio, and liked to give the impression of a childhood spent, rather grandly, travelling in his father's company. In fact, at this stage in his life (and no doubt more relevantly to his subsequent career) he did run into some pretty exotic types, but only when staying with his father in the dilapidated hotel the latter had bought at Grand Detour, Illinois: this was patronized mainly by touring vaudevillians, and from them (much to Dr Bernstein's horror) the young Welles learned the rudiments of

9

juggling, illusionism and other tricks.

His health effectively kept him out of school until he was nearly eleven, so that he had acquired a lot of cultural grounding at home from his mother and the doctor, and carried out a few tentative sexual explorations with his girl cousins in upstate New York, but had spent little time with boys of his own age and little cared to do so. But fears that he might prove ungovernable like his brother Richard, who had been expelled from school at the age of ten and subsequently banished from home, brought him in 1926 to enrolment in the Todd School for Boys at Woodstock, Illinois, a few months after his mother's death from a liver condition at the age of forty-three. The school seems to have been an eccentric enough institution in all conscience, if not necessarily ideally equipped for the nurturing of young and wayward genius. It was run by the proprietor, a terror rejoicing in the name of Noble Hill and universally known as 'the King'. New boy Orson immediately, with precocious perception, appreciated the need of a protector, and, being used to manipulating older men to get what he wanted, picked infallibly on the King's son Roger, known as Skipper, who taught athletics and coached the basketball team.

Decision was one thing, achievement another. Skipper was after all the idol of the whole school, and Orson but the youngest and least athletically capable new recruit. However, his extraordinary performance at the school's Hallowe'en concert, performing magic tricks with incomplete success disguised by fantastic aplomb, seems to have caught Skipper's attention, and from then on not only was he the boy's friend and mentor, but the most active encourager of inventiveness and creativity wherever it was to be found among the students of Todd School. Orson, for his part, sensing some hostility in Skipper's wife Hortense and his three children, set himself to slip gracefully into the family scene – no doubt he had learnt a thing or two about that from Dr Bernstein – and soon made Hortense at least a friend for

life. Among his own contemporaries, however, he is said to have had no friends – indeed, it was difficult to imagine what this small, chubby, amazingly knowledgeable adult could be doing in a place like this.

Todd School had something of a tradition in drama, though mainly lightweight revues (written and staged by Skipper), nativity plays and such. In this department, though, Orson soon got his own way. He was before long adapting, directing and starring in a long line of improbable vehicles: *Doctor Faustus*; *Everyman*; *Le Médecin Malgré Lui*; *Julius Caesar*, with Orson as Cassius (not too lean and hungry) and also Mark Antony, so that he could get all the best speeches; *Richard III*; *Dr Jekyll and Mr Hyde*, with Orson as both; *Androcles and the Lion*, with Orson as both (though how he managed that is not quite clear); the Gospel Story with Orson as (but who else?) Jesus Christ, though he might perhaps have doubled as Judas. He also built and managed a large puppet theatre, writing his own melodramatic scripts and directing his assistants with the utmost authority. No wonder an office assistant advised Skipper to 'keep a file on this kid'. No wonder Skipper did so.

As he moved into his teens Orson suddenly

shot up, developed a resonant baritone voice and, at the age of fourteen, discovered sex with a seventeen-year-old girl on board ship coming back from a holiday in Italy. From then on he took to climbing out of Todd to besiege the girls of Woodstock. And on the platonic level, there were still at least three men competing for his interest and affections (possibly this plethora of masculine affection in his youth was one reason why the adult Orson never seems to have been drawn in the slightest to homosexuality): his father, by now a hopeless alcoholic; Dadda Bernstein, still fussing over Orson's development back home in Chicago; and Skipper Hill, who was to be a dominant influence for some years to come.

The young Welles, in fact, was already well on his way to becoming a legend. Everybody seemed to be convinced that he was extraordinary, and quite possibly a genius in the making. Even his father was, though he scorned to acknowledge it and sneaked in to see his son's performances only when he was convinced no one would know he was there. The legend was augmented when the Todd production of *Julius Caesar* was entered for the annual Chicago Drama League contest and allegedly failed to win first prize only because the judges were convinced that the actors playing Cassius and Antony (Orson and Orson, both aged fourteen) must be professional adults and the production was therefore disqualified. Many thought that Orson was being outrageously spoilt with so much attention: but Orson himself always maintained that it had the opposite effect, in that everyone took it for granted he would be good, and he constantly had to cope with disappointment if he was ever less than unique.

By this time, in any case, his (non-existent) childhood was coming to an end. In the summer of 1930 his father made his last attempt to win back the boy's affections by taking him on a famous trip to China. But it was too late: they quarrelled most of the time when Welles senior was not too drunk to quarrel, and on

their return Skipper and his wife persuaded Orson not to see his father again until the latter had given up drinking. As it happened, that meant for ever, as Richard Welles died (of heart and kidney failure) in a Chicago hotel on 28 December 1930 – the doctor called in being, ironically, Dadda Bernstein, summoned as a family friend.

It proved that in his will he had directed, whether innocently or with posthumous malice, that Orson was to choose his own guardian until his majority. The obvious candidates were Bernstein and Skipper, but Orson did not feel so comfortable with Bernstein since he had married a divorced Italian opera star and lived in a household which also included the diva's ex-husband. In any case, Skipper was his mentor now, so he chose Skipper. But Skipper refused this dubious honour, and talked Orson into nominating Bernstein instead, as though he were the first choice. In a few months the question of who, precisely, was his guardian would be academic anyway.

After he had graduated from Todd at the age of sixteen, having enjoyed a resounding success in his overcrowded but enthralling encapsulation of Shakespeare histories (something he was to do again in his maturity), he was determined on an actor's life, backed if necessary with his own money. Dadda Bernstein had a fit at the idea, and was in a position to say no to the money part of it. But in compensation he packed Orson off to Europe for the summer. And there the professional career really begins.

This, of course, is the most mythologized part of all. According to Welles's version, oft repeated with elegant variation, he landed in Galway, hiked round Connemara painting for a couple of months, then went to Dublin and talked his way into a role at the famous Gate Theatre by convincing its directors, Hilton Edwards and Micheal MacLiammoir, that he was a seasoned performer with experience at the New York Theatre Guild as well as having directed, written, and toured the States as a sword-swallowing female impersonator.

11

MacLiammoir in his autobiography tells a rather different story, which should be evaluated, no doubt, in the light of Welles's later assertion that MacLiammoir was not even present at the time, being busy acting in London. He describes Welles as 'a very tall young man with a chubby face, full powerful lips, and disconcerting Chinese eyes. His hands were enormous and very beautifully shaped, like so many American hands; they were coloured like champagne and moved with a sort of controlled abandon never seen in a European.' Though, he insists, they never for a moment believed this extraordinary youth, whose 'chubby tea-rose cheeks were as satin-like as though the razor had never known them', they took him on (at amateur's wages) to play a small part in *Jew Süss*, then going into production. But they still needed an actor to play the Duke in *Jew Süss*, and, for all his obvious inexperience, Welles looked as though, if he could act at all, he might be the man. He could, and he was.

What was it that so impressed them? 'Some ageless and superb inner confidence that no one could blow out. It was unquenchable. That was his secret. He knew he was precisely what he himself would have chosen to be had God consulted him on the subject at his birth; he fully appreciated and approved what had been bestowed, and realized that he couldn't have done the job better himself, in fact he would not have changed a single item. Whether we and the world felt the same – well, that was for us to decide.'

Anyway, Welles's performance as the Duke was quite a success, putting Hilton Edwards's as the Jew somewhat in the shade – or so several critics suggested, though criticism of Irish theatre in Ireland at the time was inclined to be indulgent, and Welles was, after all, a new face. Though he stayed on at the Gate from October 1931 to February 1932, and appeared in six productions, the Duke was the nearest he came to playing a lead, and in one or two of the others he was virtually invisible. Not surprising, one would think, in view of his very junior position in the company. However, Welles himself seems to have retained his capacity to be surprised, and even half a century later he was still hinting darkly at homosexual jealousy on MacLiammoir's part over his (platonic, filial) relationship with Edwards as the cause. We may admit at least that it is very unlikely either of them would risk being outshone in their own company – if either felt the danger, that is – and any latterday rationalization based on personal malice would seem to be discounted by the evident and continuing friendship between Welles and the two directors of the Gate in a variety of later collaborations. By and large, the sojourn in Ireland seems to have been a good thing for Welles, building up his confidence in his own abilities as a performer (if any building-up were needed) and, more importantly, bringing him into contact, through Edwards, with relatively avant-garde European ideas of the theatre, far removed from the basic realism which was still orthodoxy even in New York. Welles was a quick learner, as he was to show in his own first professional productions.

Once he left the Gate, Welles does not seem to have had any very specific ideas of what he wanted to do. He went to London, hoping for

 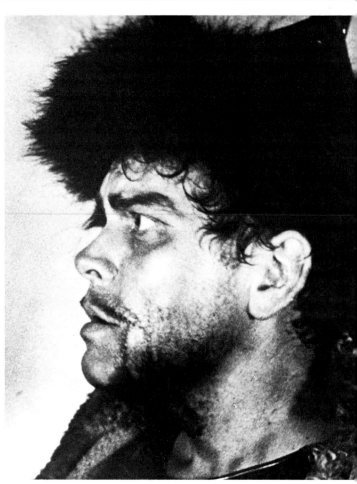

work, but could not get the necessary British work permit. So he decided to return to the States, confidently expecting to find a job in New York. But alas, no one had ever heard of him, he could not get past the doorman at the Schuberts' all powerful theatrical management, and back he went almost at once to Illinois, which might not be so glamorous, but at least was more comfortable, and full of confirmed admirers.

Skipper Hill had now taken over Todd School from his father, and Welles was at once taken on as drama coach ('I've always had the job of keeping this guy busy and out of my hair,' Skipper said later) and director of an edited *Twelfth Night* for the 1932 Chicago Drama Festival, in which Todd this year won first prize. After that the Hills established Welles in Chicago, in a flat in Old Town, where he worked on the first four volumes of the series *Everybody's Shakespeare*, edited 'by Roger Hill and Orson Welles', though in fact Skipper was responsible for the text and Welles for the illustrations and the essay 'On Staging Shakespeare and on Shakespeare's Stage'. Five years later, in 1939, Harpers put out these four volumes again as *The Mercury Shakespeare*, the editors' billing reversed (exploiting Welles's subsequent success with the Mercury Theatre), and as such they stayed in print until 1964.

Meanwhile, through the Hills, Welles made another valuable contact: at a party in a Todd parent's house, he met the playwright Thornton Wilder. For a wonder, Wilder had even heard of him and his Dublin success (or so Welles later averred), and after a few nights spent drinking with the lad wrote him letters of recommendation to his friend Alexander Woollcott, who in his turn handed Welles on to Guthrie McClintic, producer-director and husband of Katharine Cornell. McClintic and Cornell were just preparing a national tour taking three plays coast-to-coast: *The Barretts of Wimpole Street*, *Romeo and Juliet* and *Candida*. Welles was hired, without even a proper audition, to play the stuttering brother Octavius in *The Barretts* (a very minor role), Mercutio in *Romeo* (a shortish but showy role) and, astonishingly, the lead role of Marchbanks opposite Katharine Cornell in *Candida*. 'Looks rather like the saga has begun,' he wrote excitedly to Skipper that night. And so in a sense it had. At least Welles survived the seven-month tour, despite making enemies by his taste for childish pranks off-stage (perhaps making up belatedly for the childhood he had never had) and his tendency to seem lazy, big-headed and offensively superior towards the rest of the company. He was already reputed to be difficult to direct (he and McClintic never really hit it off) and in the opinion of other cast-members he was poor as Octavius, obviously considering the role beneath him, passable if undistinguished as Mercutio (being demoted from that role to Tybalt later in the tour) and interesting only as Marchbanks, for which role he was wrong in everything but age – he should have been slight, delicate and 'almost unearthly', instead of which he was big, booming and wild, but somehow generated enough excitement for it to work.

If the McClintic-Cornells were not entirely ecstatic about their noisy cuckoo in the nest, he was far from pleased with them – especially when he heard that they were putting off their promised season in New York till the autumn of 1934, filling in with an unscheduled tour of the South. Since his Broadway début had been an important bait, he began to look elsewhere for something to do. At which, he sprang upon the unsuspecting Skipper the notion of a summer festival at Woodstock, arranged by him and starring, in addition to himself, none other than Michael MacLiammoir and Hilton Edwards from Dublin, the first to offer his Hamlet, the second to play *Czar Paul*, and Welles to do something he would think of later. A little dubiously, but still eager to keep Welles happy, Skipper agreed to underwrite the festival to the tune of $2,000, if Welles could, as he promised, raise the other $1,000 necessary. On guarded consideration, MacLiammoir

17

and Edwards agreed too, and the Woodstock
Summer Festival Theatre was in business.

What Welles elected to do for himself was
Trilby, playing of course a bearded, saturnine,
thoroughly over-the-top Svengali. MacLiammoir and Edwards did what had been predicted
for them, and MacLiammoir's Hamlet in particular (Welles played Claudius and the Ghost)
was adjudged not unworthy of its reputation
as currently the best in the world (this was, after
all, a few months before Gielgud). But in any
case, if the festival was successful enough not
actually to lose money, it was not so much the
critics' doing as the inspired advice Skipper
received from a friend to ignore the critics and
make sure the shows were constantly in the
social columns instead: then and since, such

enterprises were likely to do a lot better if they
were the 'in' thing to do than they were if they
merely promised art and enlightenment. The
unorthodox amatory exploits of the visitors
amazed (and apparently delighted) the locals,
the society columns were full of silly stories
about débutantes and dowagers, and the whole
affair went off with quite a satisfactory bang.

Scarcely more than a whisper on the side-
lines that summer was Welles's other venture:
no less than his first film, *The Hearts of Age*.
It is rather too grand even to describe it that
way: Welles himself said it was 'not a film at
all – just a little joke one Sunday afternoon.'
A bare four minutes of edited film (16mm), it
is a collage of unrelated images, vaguely gothic
in feeling, and it is not even clear, as with so
many amateur ventures, who did what in it. It
features Welles himself, a pretty young
débutante called Virginia Nicolson, who had
excited the social columnists by understudying
in *Czar Paul*, and even getting to play the role
one night, and a friend called William Vance,
who actually seems to have shot the film,
mostly from 'happenings mainly invented by
Orson over a drink'. Enthusiastic Welles-
watchers, who can seek out the film at
Greenwich Public Library, can sometimes be
persuaded that it bears the master touch, but
most find it more interesting as a documentary
insight on his early years and ideas, conveyed
largely by putting together his drawings and
the stagings of what was drawn. It has an added
significance in that shortly after it was shot
Virginia Nicolson became the first Mrs Orson
Welles.

The romance had begun when she audi-
tioned for the festival and chose a speech from
Henry IV part one. She was spectacularly
pretty, looked incredibly dainty and fragile
next to Orson's shambling bulk, had perfect
manners and dress sense from her wealthy
upbringing, and moreover had an unexpected
streak of fantasy that Orson found enchanting.
They got on well together, but did not, at least
according to Orson, take the relationship all

that seriously. Indeed, he insisted, they decided to get married only so that they could live together without question in a New York hotel. The wedding was hurried and conspiratorial, with only Skipper and Hortense Hill invited; but when the Nicolsons and Dadda Bernstein found out it had happened they rapidly insisted on a more formal re-run before the thing could be publicly admitted to. And meanwhile Welles was busy preparing for his first Broadway opening.

That was the point of the New York hotel. After the Woodstock Festival Welles had rejoined the Katharine Cornell company, only to find that in the interim Brian Aherne had been signed to play Browning in *The Barretts of Wimpole Street*, and had insisted on, or been persuaded into (accounts differ), playing Mercutio as well. So now Welles was given the lesser role of Tybalt, as well as opening the play as the Chorus. Well, it could have been better, but it could easily have been worse. At least it was definitely Broadway, at the Martin Beck Theatre on 20 December 1934. And, he was good as Tybalt – decidedly better, most people thought, than he had been as Mercutio. Moreover, on the second night he was seen and admired by someone who was to be his next and in many ways most important father-figure, mentor and guide: none other than the director, producer, teacher, autobiographer and eventually star actor John Houseman. The eventual meeting was going to be fateful for them both.

*The words
of Mercury*

2

AS JOHN HOUSEMAN TELLS IT, WITH A FINE dramatic flourish, in the first volume of his autobiography, for him it was fascination, if not exactly love, at first sight. What he saw in Welles, at least as Tybalt, was little short of demonic. But also absorbing. Houseman wanted to work with this man. Warily he circled for a week or two, nurturing his own obsession. Then finally he approached. Now Houseman at this time was thirty-two – thirteen years older than Welles and not unknown in New York artistic circles: he had had a considerable *succès d'estime* earlier in the year directing the first production of the Virgil Thomson / Gertrude Stein opera *Four Saints in Three Acts*. He was a young man of whom much was expected. And as far as Welles was concerned he had the impressive cosmopolitan background – Romanian-born, English public-school-educated – which could inspire confidence and emulation. And he had a concrete offer in mind for this 'monstrous boy': he was preparing a three-night-only presentation of Archibald MacLeish's boldly political play *Panic*, and having failed to interest Paul Muni or any other established actor in playing the lead, he thought Welles would be just right for the job.

Welles thought so too – he would be finished with Tybalt by then, and it was a Broadway lead, if only for three nights. But typically, he played it cool – the emotional tug-of-war which was always to be a feature of his relationship with Houseman was already beginning. In addition, Virginia (with whom he had now moved to a bleak Riverside Drive studio apartment) did not like Houseman, or maybe was jealous of Welles's new obsessive interest. But the job could bring him just the kind of attention and contacts he wanted, Welles sagely reflected, and continued to work in his spare time on a play called *Bright Lucifer*, in which he and other figures of his childhood appeared interestingly caricatured – himself not least as the difficult and devilishly manipulative teenage boy who precipitates the eventual serio-comic disaster. Whether this proves that Welles possessed at this time extraordinary self-knowledge, and deliberately fostered Houseman's picturesquely fiendish image of him, is of course another matter entirely.

Whatever the truth about Welles at this juncture – and one can only at one's peril discount the estimate of so acute a judge as John Houseman – there is no doubting the fruitfulness of the new collaboration. Welles did indeed get good reviews for his performance in *Panic*, even if he did not endear himself to the left-wing intellectuals who gathered round the enterprise by openly scoffing at their solemnity. The short run over, he determined not to come down to anything less than a lead for his next Broadway appearance, and settled himself to wait, supported by some intermittent radio work and regular handouts from Skipper. A wandering summer achieved little, apart from completion of the never-produced *Bright Lucifer*, but then, come autumn, Welles suddenly found that he was the radio actor most in demand, and could make as much money as he liked from his ability to assume all accents and ages in the otherwise tiresome anonymity of innumerable plays and documentaries and features during this 'golden age' of radio.

Useful as that was – and it was not the last time his voice would be his fortune, right up to his last days when he lived primarily off providing the voice of endless television commercials – what he really needed was a project. And shortly before his twenty-first birthday, just such a project materialized – from a rather unlikely quarter. With the Roosevelt government's programme to counteract the effects of the Depression came encouragement for the arts (artists had to work and live just like anyone else) through the Works Progress Administration (WPA), which promptly set up various federally funded 'projects', among them the Federal Theatre Project. The first director of the project was eager to encourage experimental and minority theatre rather than Broadway, which even in those difficult days

seemed able to look after itself. In New York the most obvious minority was black, and so a Negro Theatre was at once set up in Harlem, co-directed by Rose MacClendon, a noted black actress, and – John Houseman, whose experience with the all-black *Four Saints in Three Acts* obviously stood him in good stead. Here was the opportunity Houseman had been waiting for to work again, more extensively, with the boy genius, and so the hunt was on for some suitably sensational way of setting him to work.

The Harlem Theatre's programme provided, of course, for the production of new plays on specifically black themes, but also for all-black reinterpretations of world classics. Virginia Welles is generally credited with the idea of a 'Voodoo *Macbeth*', setting the play as it might be on Haiti in the time of the black emperor Henri Christophe, a contemporary of Napoleon and model for Eugene O'Neill's *Emperor Jones*. And as soon as the idea was floated, Welles himself was quick to see how, with a little bit of cutting and rearrangement, the play could fit into this setting. The way it worked out was that the fully professional production side was all white – Welles, Virginia as his assistant, Abe Feder in charge of the all-

important lighting, Nat Karson designing the
luxuriant sub-tropical sets, Virgil Thomson
composing and arranging the music – while the
performers, naturally, were all black. Though
the four principals were seasoned professionals
(backed up by numerous amateurs and semi-
professionals), it was predictable that none of
them had had any experience of playing
Shakespeare before: Jack Carter, who played
Macbeth, had been the original Crown in
Porgy, the play upon which *Porgy and Bess* was
based; Edna Thomas, the Lady Macbeth, had
had a substantial career playing black mam-
mies in plays about white folks; Canada Lee,
the Banquo, had formerly been a professional
boxer; and Eric Burroughs, who played
Hecate, a character largely cooked up by
Welles from the witches' scene as a voodoo

MAC DUFF

priest with a bullwhip, was a graduate of
London's Royal Academy of Dramatic Art.
Otherwise, virtually anyone who could read
lines was recruited.

In the circumstances, it was not to be expected that the young director, in the limited time
at his disposal, would be able to get very subtle
and detailed performances out of the actors. In
any case, that was not really, or was ever to
be, his kind of theatre: primed with his own,
vaguely Gordon Craig-derived ideas of the
director as superman and the actors as puppets
in his control, as well as with Hilton Edwards's
more practical notions about the primacy of
the overall theatrical gesture, he set out to
make the show an exciting succession of sounds
and images, working on its audience more like
an opera or a ballet than a reasoned reading
of the text. With all the over-confident inse-
curity of his twenty years, he tyrannized over
his technical staff, more or less forbade Houseman the theatre on the grounds that occasional
attendance at rehearsals was distracting, and
was persuaded not to be too tough with his
touchy actors only by his leading lady's point-
ing out that if he was too openly disdainful of
their efforts they might always cut him up. (As
it was, he nearly got badly slashed by a black
activist convinced that the *Macbeth* production
could be designed only to hold the black community up to hatred, ridicule and contempt.)

The rehearsals, consequently, were chaos –
but the kind of just-controlled chaos in which
Welles was always to function most effectively.
If no one else knew what the hell was going
on, the more complete was his control as the
only authority and saviour of the day. And the
element of risk obviously turned him on,
encouraging him to make a superhuman effort
and snatch victory out of the jaws of defeat.
Victory the *Macbeth* certainly was, despite
mumbles from the conservative Press about the
quality of the verse-speaking. Perry Hammond
in the *Herald Tribune* deplored 'the inability
of so noble a race to sing the music of
Shakespeare'. It was accepted, even by some

23

doubters, as a uniquely exciting evening in the theatre. John Mason Brown in the *New York Post*, for example, though generally unfavourable, found the witches' scene 'logical and stirring and a triumph of theatre art'. And the star of the occasion was the one man who never appeared on stage (except for one evening on tour when the drink-inclined Jack Carter's replacement suddenly went missing and he had to black up for the role): the director and creator, Orson Welles. Probably he was not so wide of the mark (anticipating as he did the auteur theory and 'the director as superstar' by two or three decades) when in 1939 he said that 'At about the same time in the history of the theatre that the director came in, the old-time star went out. The horrible truth is that nobody has read the last chapter of the detective story and discovered that the old-time star did not go out. He merely sits in the fifth row now and is the director.'

Whether or not Welles most wanted to be an old-time star actor or a new-fangled star director hardly matters: probably he wanted both, he wanted everything. And very soon he was going to get it. But there was also no doubt some rueful truth in his later remark that one morning he observed himself in the mirror and decided that one great advantage was that no one cared how a director looked. And after all, a director was more like a total creator than an actor could ever be. In addition to which, he was now famous as a director, and clearly it was that upon which he must initially build. He rejected an offer to take the black *Macbeth* to London, and instead moved into his own personal toy, courtesy of the Federal Theatre Project: at the Maxine Elliott Theatre he and Houseman were to inaugurate the WPA's Classical Unit. Houseman says that he recognized the necessity to channel Welles's 'terrible energy and boundless ambition' before anyone else did.

The 'classical unit' was rapidly christened Project 891 (its label on the government's books), which might look mysterious but at least did not sound stodgy. And any notion that it might be severely doctrinaire and left-wing, like so much of the work funded by the WPA, was also rapidly put to rest. Neither Houseman nor Welles was noticeably political, and it was a deliberate gesture that the season opened with a farce, Welles's own adaptation of the classic play by Labiche and Michel, *Un Chapeau de Paille d'Italie* (*The Italian Straw Hat*), as *Horse Eats Hat*. To be precise, the English text was the work of Edwin Denby, who translated, and Welles, who retranslated into workable theatrical dialogue – after which Welles proceeded during production to cut, elaborate and incorporate a lot of sight-gags. The setting was left as nominally Paris, but all the characters were given American names, and it was quite evidently set in fact in just such a small American town as Welles had known as a child. The action of Labiche's play was followed quite closely – a horse belonging to the hero eats a hat belonging to a lady romping in the bushes with someone she ought not to be, and the rest of the play concerns the young man's frantic attempts to replace the hat during what is scheduled to be his wedding day. But Welles was inspired more by René Clair's silent film of the play and, nearer home, by Marx Brothers movies than by the kind of theatrical treatment usual at that time.

On this occasion he did not have to adopt this approach in order to disguise the shortcomings of his cast: the WPA's ruling that the out-of-work and amateur actors in their productions could be leavened by ten per cent of working professionals enabled Welles to cast such as Joseph Cotten (to be an important associate for long afterwards), Arlene Francis, Hiram Sherman and of course himself, alternating with his old Todd friend Edgerton Paul as the opinionated businessman Mortimer J. Mugglethorpe, a character seemingly inspired by his own father. His wife Virginia was also in the cast, and on the technical side he had gathered together again the *Macbeth* team of Feder, Karson and Thomson, this time with author-composer Paul Bowles to write the music Thomson arranged and orchestrated. Just as much as *Macbeth*, it was an essay in total theatre, though with rather less justification, many felt, in that the humour of the original slight, fast-moving farce was slowed down and submerged by too many showy extravagances, too much noise and colour and too little economy of effect. Not for the last time, Welles was accused of lacking self-discipline. But then again, some influential people (particularly in the loftier arty set) liked it very much, and staunch supporters would go every night to chant the lines in unison with the actors, much as a later generation would do with *The Rocky Horror Show*.

And all the while Welles, ever a glutton for work, was busy with other things. He was still constantly doing radio – something which, as well as making him enough money to live comfortably, above the level of the WPA's

25

subsistence-wages, did undoubtedly help to tune his extraordinary sensitivity to the effect of sheer sound in the theatre and cinema. He had also agreed to star in Sidney Kingsley's well-meaning but uninspiring anti-war drama *Ten Million Ghosts*. Why this was, no one could tell, since he detested Kingsley (troubles with taking direction again), had no great admiration for the play, and had to leave the cast of *Horse Eats Hat* in order to rehearse and play the role. Though not for long: the play closed almost as soon as it opened, and he was back with *Horse Eats Hat* again for the rest of the New York run.

Macbeth had been a dazzling improvisation out of practically nothing, *Horse Eats Hat* a surrealist romp which irritated as many as it delighted. The next production had to be the clincher, the serious success which would transform Welles from an enfant terrible into a fully fledged adult genius. After all, time was rushing by: he was already twenty-one! And so, not

without some agonizing, Welles selected for his third WPA venture Christopher Marlowe's Elizabethan morality play *Doctor Faustus*. The text of this, a short play anyway, he had again cut to the bone, so that the whole evening's entertainment ran a bare seventy minutes without a break, from 9.00 to 10.10 – this, he said, apart from his own impatience and his cynical assessment of the audience's patience with a gloomy classic, was due to his need to do a regular radio broadcast twice a week at 8.00 before a studio audience, and then return to do it again for Pacific zone listeners at 11.00. He was also, to swell the coffers, doing a regular weekly stint on radio in one of his famous roles, Cranston Lamont, 'the Shadow', who knew all and constantly unmasked criminals and righted wrongs.

Which was just as well, because he frequently found himself subsidizing the WPA shows with up to $1,000 a week of his own money – or so he later claimed, and it may well be so. Certainly that and his ill-concealed impatience with government bureaucracy did not make him the most governable person on the WPA's books, and there were those who disliked and distrusted him even if he did appear to get results. The production of *Doctor Faustus*, relatively severe on a bare thrust stage draped in black velvet, with himself as Faust and Jack Carter, temporarily weaned from the bottle, as Mephistopheles, was one of those results: it got generally decent notices, was praised for its imagination if still castigated for the poor quality of its elocution, particularly in the verse, and ran for an amazing sixteen weeks.

But Welles's big clash with his government employers was just around the corner. Working for the WPA was like walking a tightrope. On the one hand your work was supposed to be serious and socially responsible – a criterion which *Horse Eats Hat* scarcely satisfied. On the other hand seriousness and social responsibility were not supposed to lead to anything actually controversial, let alone revolutionary. So it was not a wise move when, having met

27

and been enchanted by the communist playwright-composer Marc Blitzstein, Welles agreed to put on his manifesto-opera, *The Cradle Will Rock*, in a full Broadway-style production, and then, if it was successful, run it in alternation with *Doctor Faustus* for an indefinite run. Welles had had a taste of opera direction already by staging the premiere three performances of Aaron Copland's opera for children *The Second Hurricane* (libretto by his *Horse Eats Hat* collaborator Edwin Denby) at the Henry Street Settlement Music School, and seems to have been eager to follow up the theatrical possibilities of the form rather than being inspired by Blitzstein's message of unionization – now. But the fact that the show would be heavily supported by the influential and organized left-wing intellectual audience in New York cannot have failed entirely to enter into his and Houseman's calculations.

Everything seemed to be going smoothly with the preparation of the show, until the WPA back in Washington got wind of its revolutionary intent. The opening was scheduled for 21 June 1937, but on 11 June the administration were informed that there were to be cuts in finance and general changes of staffing at the WPA, and meanwhile nothing new was to open until the next financial year, which started in July. Undeterred, Welles went on working towards the preview, hoping apparently to bring about a government change of heart. But after an invitation-only preview on 14 June, guards were brought in to seal the theatre and officially lock Welles and his company out. This involved a number of technicalities militating against production elsewhere: Equity said that its members could not in the circumstances appear on stage in a show closed by the management, and there was no way to get the elaborate settings and props out of the Maxine Elliott Theatre. But Welles, up to now undecided what to do, was confirmed in his resolve by opposition, and also saw the news-possibilities of this off-stage drama. A frantic search found an empty

theatre – the old Venice, some thirty blocks uptown – and Welles improvised a form of presentation in which only Blitzstein would be on stage, playing a piano and telling the story, while the actors, not permitted 'on stage', would materialize in the audience to sing their roles, picked out by Feder's wandering spotlights.

It was all very dramatic, controversial and moving, playing its first preview as planned (and only an hour or so late) before – and among – a packed audience. The newspapers made a meal of it; everyone loves a rebel; and the whole thing was, of course, a wild success, if the sort of success which can very easily lead to nothing but the dole-queue. Welles was not too nonplussed. He still had his lucrative, if not deeply satisfying, radio work to support him. Virginia was pregnant. And the big-time Broadway producer Arthur Hopkins offered him the chance to star in *King Lear* on Broadway that autumn. King Lear, at an age when almost any other actor you can think of would still be expecting to play Romeo . . . Unfortunately, the intended production fell through, from lack of funds, and as second-best Welles got together with Houseman, also by now fired from the WPA, to set up as quickly as they could a viable commercial (but yet artistic) company for the impending autumn. On 29 August readers of *The New York Times* were startled by a 'declaration of principles' on the front page of the Drama Section, from something hitherto unheard-of called The Mercury Theatre. Now that they had principles and a policy (mixed classics, low prices, no particular political commitment), all they needed was a theatre and a little money to get started.

Almost immediately, both of these were secured, the theatre being the Comedy on West 41st Street, and Welles began preparing the first two productions, a modern-dress *Julius Caesar* evoking the brutal pageantry of Hitler's Germany and Mussolini's Italy, and Dekker's Elizabethan working-class comedy *The Shoemaker's Holiday*. In order to stress the

modern parallels in Shakespeare, Welles cut and rearranged his text even more mercilessly than usual, though there seems to have been surprisingly little comment on the fact – presumably because reviewers were swept away by the theatrical exhilaration of it all. In contrast to his famous schoolboy double-act as Cassius and Antony, Welles himself here played the moderate, civilized and therefore finally ineffectual Brutus, distinguished from the rest of the cast by his immaculately tailored suits. In his own performance, as in so much else, his concept was primarily visual. He thought in pictures, then fitted the human details – as far as they could be fitted – into them. It was theatricalist, non-realistic theatre, with psychological niceties going by the board. Therefore, what everybody who saw the early productions seems to remember is not the acting, or what they were about, but how they

looked. In *Julius Caesar*, the upward beams of light from spots concealed in the floor (an idea borrowed from newsreels of Nazi rallies in Nuremberg) and the bare blood-red wall at the back, counted for much more than any logical argument – indeed, Welles, in his advertised opposition to European fascism, was making excellent use of the enemy's own weapons to achieve a kindred effect, going straight to the instincts and emotions rather than filtering its message through the mind.

For all his undoubted intelligence, Welles was never an intellectual, in the theatre or out of it. He was a quick reactor, a brilliant improviser, a vivid visualizer, but he seldom cared to stop and think, and hardly ever gave his audiences time to do the same. In a way, the live theatre was his ideal medium, the perfect form for the prestidigitator's magic, since you never see exactly the same thing twice. It is surprising that he was later to make films which could stand up triumphantly to the most minute and frequent analysis, but that (despite overtures already from Warner Brothers to go and act in the movies) was still on the distant horizon for this young man in a hurry. Cutting and changing and rearranging to the very last (the play never ended twice the same way throughout the rehearsals and previews), Welles ended up with the nearest he had yet come to a total triumph when *Julius Caesar* opened on 11 November 1937, and even writing forty years later the producer Norman Lloyd recalled that 'it was the definitive Mercury production in its supreme theatricality.'

There is a vexed question here about how much of the production (this and others) Welles was directly, personally responsible for. Certainly at the time he claimed – or had claimed for him – total responsibility for the concept and a lot of the detailed working out, with the unobtrusively credited designers, lighting directors and such only realizing his ideas and doing his bidding. From a publicity point of view if nothing else this was desirable: nothing must diminish the saleable image of the young genius. Later there have been undignified and now quite unverifiable squabbles over who really did what, and undeniably some of his closest collaborators feel a continuing sense of grievance. Notwithstanding, a Welles stage production always looked like a Welles stage production and nothing else, just as a Welles film is always unmistakably a Welles film, in its grandeurs and its follies. To say that he always needed a back-up team of talent and skill almost matching his own is not to diminish in any way (indeed, in a sense it may actually augment) one's assessment of his genius in co-ordinating them all and bending all their individual gifts to his vision of the possible in the midst of what to everyone else was unthinkable.

The Shoemaker's Holiday was due to open on New Year's Day 1938, but as if preparing that and playing *Julius Caesar* were not enough, the Mercury revived *The Cradle Will Rock* as a 'Worklight Theatre' production on Sunday nights only, that being *Julius Caesar's* dark night. All the same, *The Shoemaker's Holiday* was ready early – early enough for Welles to take the unprecedented step of asking any of the *Julius Caesar* audience who wanted to stay on after the Christmas Eve performance to sit in on the dress rehearsal of the Dekker, which was due immediately afterwards and did not finish until 2.30 Christmas morning. The situation was so dramatic, and so typically Wellesian, that most did stay, and responded with such enthusiasm that Welles could reasonably expect another hit. So in fact it proved: Welles had again cut, rearranged and rewritten his original to turn it into a slightly bawdy but fundamentally sentimental comedy which Americans accustomed to the soft-centred social-realist film comedies of Frank Capra could wholeheartedly appreciate, and in doing so deftly got both critics and audiences on his side. Also, the critics noted, the actual acting in Mercury productions was getting better. John Mason Brown, in the *New York Post*, applauded Welles for attracting an 'increasingly impressive list of actors who with reason and the theatre's best interests at heart, have rallied under his conquering banner'. Even if in rehearsal the actors resented being treated like marionettes and being made to jump to numbers, Welles's control of the whole concept was such that in performance they came up, or seemed to come up, with fresh, idiosyncratic and touchingly human characterizations.

So Welles had reason to feel satisfied. *The Shoemaker's Holiday* ran successfully at the Comedy; *Julius Caesar* went on tour; *The Cradle Will Rock* moved to the Windsor Theatre, where it could play nightly. Then *The Shoemaker's Holiday* was a big enough hit to move to a larger theatre, the National, so *The Cradle Will Rock* moved back to the Comedy. Three hits in three months was not bad going, even by the standards Welles set himself. The

31

Opposite: Welles delighted in playing an old man when barely into his twenties, and did it to spectacular effect as Captain Shotover in his uncharacteristically straightforward production of Shaw's *Heartbreak House* with Geraldine Fitzgerald as Ellie Dunn. Below: in the CBS studio, still in his *Heartbreak House* makeup, after one of his mad dashes from stage to radio. Left: more normally dressed, directing one of his Mercury Theatre on the Air productions.

only question was, what next? Welles wanted to have another go at his Shakespearian Wars-of-the-Roses compilation, under the title *Five Kings*, but he proved unable to boil it down to less than two nights' theatre, so it was laid aside. Next *The Duchess of Malfi* was announced, but cancelled the next day, when Welles fully realized that the play needed a fine classically trained company and would not be amenable to his usual forms of manipulation. Next he decided to diversify by assigning a production to another director, and *Measure for Measure* was set in motion under the direction of Hiram 'Chubby' Sherman, who was having a great personal success as an actor in *The Shoemaker's Holiday*. After some weeks of rehearsal the production was cancelled without explanation – something which no doubt hastened Sherman's 'treacherous' departure from the company in favour of Broadway fame and fortune.

But the question of a final production for the Mercury's season was becoming urgent. And suddenly, out of the blue, Welles, who could always be expected to do the unexpected, announced that he had cabled George Bernard Shaw for the American rights of *Heartbreak House*, and Shaw had agreed – with the proviso, difficult for Welles to stomach, that the text must not be cut or interfered with in any way. Well, probably it was about time that Welles and the Mercury faced the ultimate challenge by showing that they could if need be play it straight. Paradoxically that, which would be the norm for any other company, became the great talking-point of the new production, and Welles again garnered golden opinions, both for his restrained and stylish direction and for his own performance, heavily disguised, as the octogenarian Captain Shotover. Just before the play opened, Welles became the father of a daughter, perversely christened Christopher; a couple of months later he made the cover of *Time*. Who would not feel happy?

Why, Orson Welles, of course. His second

season with the Mercury had to outdo the first. And meanwhile he was going into his busiest period ever on radio, which would occupy him and the major players from the Mercury Theatre regularly in hour-long weekly dramas adapted, produced and directed by Welles under the collective titles of, successively, *First Person Singular*, *The Mercury Theatre on the Air* and *The Campbell Playhouse* (all for CBS) from 11 July 1938 to 2 June 1939, and again from 10 September 1939 until 31 March 1940. In these series he worked with a number of his later Hollywood stalwarts such as actors Joseph Cotten, Everett Sloane, Ray Collins, Paul Stewart and Agnes Moorehead, all of whom were in *Citizen Kane*, as well as composer Bernard Herrmann and writer Herman J. Mankiewicz, who both also worked on *Kane*. As well as all this, he was preparing the Mercury's second season due to begin in November. But this time the auguries were not good. At home Welles's marriage was not going well, and his philandering became more and more open. He seemed no longer to be seeing eye-to-eye with John Houseman, his partner in the Mercury enterprise. And the difficulties in finding suitable material with which to wow New York even more completely than the first season had done seemed to augment from day to day. Perhaps Welles – even he – was overworked. Perhaps, ever mercurial, he had lost interest, or was shortly to do so.

And then there were the matters over which he could have no control. The departure of Hiram Sherman meant the sudden cancellation of a sensible idea, to try out during the summer a new production of *The Importance of Being Earnest* (to star Sherman, of course) which would open the New York season in alternation with a revival of *The Shoemaker's Holiday*. Next Welles and Houseman planned to open with another, more dramatic alternation, starting on consecutive nights to garner maximum publicity. It would consist of *Too Much Johnson*, a *Horse Eats Hat* type of entertainment freely adapted by Welles from an old American farce by William Gillette, and Georg Büchner's stark drama of the French Revolution *Danton's Death*, with which, in a much rewritten version, Max Reinhardt had had a spectacular American success ten years before. There were obvious drawbacks to each half of this projected double, but maybe the combination would fire imaginations ...

And at least *Too Much Johnson* would be tried out at a summer theatre in upstate New York, run by a couple of Mercury graduates. To enliven it and open it out, Welles planned to shoot a filmed prologue on the streets of New York. And at that point, maybe, the die was cast. Once Welles began working seriously with this new toy, the cinema, he became totally absorbed in it, shooting more and more and teaching himself the tricks of the trade as he went along. In film, it seemed, he found the infinitely flexible, malleable, adaptable medium he had always been looking for in the theatre. And from that moment, Barbara Leaming suggests, in her authorized biography, the die was cast for Welles to turn his major hopes and ambitions towards the cinema. It is a neat theory, but need not necessarily be therefore untrue. Certainly he seems to have lost interest in the staged part of *Too Much Johnson*: the film was never finished or edited (indeed, owing to money problems some of it did not even come back from the labs), and so left a hole in the show which could never be satisfactorily filled by under-rehearsed, panicked actors. Houseman vetoed it as even a possibility for New York, and Welles does not seem to have argued the point. And how about the film, this famous first (or, considering *The Heart of Age*, almost-first) Wellesian venture into the medium? Welles always dismissed the question and minimized its importance, at any rate until what appeared to be the only copy was destroyed in a fire at his Spanish villa in 1970. Thereafter, he grandly let it be supposed that it *might* have been a lost masterpiece!

This left the not very happy company stuck

34

with *Danton's Death*, suggested by the actor Martin Gabel, who was to play the title role. Now the main difficulty with *Danton's Death* is that it is not a very good play, despite a scattering of extraordinary scenes. And it does not suggest any easy, comfortable solutions, such as might make it acceptable to a large popular audience. Welles might have transformed it, as he had most of his other texts – after all, even Reinhardt produced his own text by combining Büchner with another play on a kindred theme by Romain Rolland, and then garnished it with overwhelming spectacle far beyond the Mercury's resources. But in the event Welles seems not to have bothered to do much with it, though his staging, implying the presence of the crowd rather than showing it, was among his most inventive and took his theatre as far as it was ever to go along the path of Expressionism.

Before the play even opened it seemed an air of impending doom hung over the rehearsals, no one feeling that it was going right or knowing what to do about it. At the end of October, however, The Mercury Theatre on the Air (as it then was) produced a spectacular diversion, in the shape of the notorious 'panic broadcast'. This, as the world now knows, was an adaptation by Howard Koch of H. G. Wells's *The War of the Worlds*, a suitable enough subject, it was felt, for Hallowe'en. A lot of the secret of its effect – and a lot of the argument about whether the effect was planned or not – resides in its placing in the radio schedules. The Mercury Theatre had been placed by CBS against the almost unbeatable competition of the Edgar Bergen and Charlie McCarthy show on Sunday nights. Apparently the likelihood that Charlie McCarthy fans might switch to CBS in the middle depended on the quality of the week's guest star; anyway, relatively few were listening to the Mercury show right from the beginning. And so, though this show began with the usual staid credits, the verisimilitude of what followed might be expected (or so it was subsequently claimed) to take listeners in

Two glimpses of Welles in the radio studio, one with his
trusty pipe, both intensely concentrated.

Two glimpses of Welles in the radio studio, one with his
trusty pipe, both intensely concentrated.

and convince them that they were really listening to hot news of the Martians invading New
Jersey.

Unlikely as it seems now – and it gets ever
more difficult to disentangle what really happened from journalistic exaggeration –
thousands of people seem to have believed just
that. The format of the programme was a lot
of innocuous dance music interrupted by ever
more urgent and horrific news flashes from the
scene of the supposed landing, plus interven-
tions by Welles himself as a rather excitable
astronomer. Good fun for Hallowe'en, to be
taken with a large pinch of salt. Or so one
would have imagined any sane listener might
think – even if it did not momentarily occur
to him to check whether this extraordinary
news was on any other channel. All the same,
the panic rush for shelter, the heart attacks, the
suicide attempts, the miscarriages and such
that the broadcast occasioned seem to be well
attested, and the result was that on 31 October
1938, Orson Welles woke up to find himself
internationally famous – or notorious –
beyond even his wildest dreams; certainly, if
as he later said, his only idea going into the
show was: 'Let's do something impossible,
make them believe it, then show them it's only
radio.'

Even all the publicity could not save *Danton's Death*, which opened on 2 November to
generally poor reviews (Brooks Atkinson being
the only dissenting voice) and closed after
twenty-one performances, thereby marking the
effective end of the Mercury Theatre. It is not
in any case clear how the company would have
carried on if *Danton's Death* had been a success. The *Five Kings* entertainment which continued to preoccupy Welles was clearly too big
for the Mercury's resources, and already that
summer Houseman had made a separate deal
with Theatre Guild for himself and Welles to
present it, properly on Broadway, as part of
the Guild's well-financed winter subscription
series, so some theatrical future was in view for
Welles whether the Mercury Theatre continued

or not. Working back in Woodstock, Welles managed at last to reduce the material to something like a one-night show, mainly by concentrating it (like his much later compilation *Chimes at Midnight*) on the fortunes of Prince Hal and of Falstaff, whom he would play himself. Indeed, it is no longer clear who the five kings might have been, since the cast-list of the text finally produced mentions only two, Henry IV and Henry V.

The most likely explanation of the manifold troubles with *Five Kings*, which finally drove Welles (were any driving really needed) into the arms of Hollywood, is that while Welles had the overall concept fairly clear in his head from the start, he began to work out the precise theatrical mechanics of it only when he got on to an actual stage. Much of the idea literally turned on a revolving stage, which was supposed to provide natural, split-second transitions from one scene and location to another. But the revolve never worked right, and the easy running of the play was fatally sabotaged. (A year or two later the famously disastrous Laurence Olivier / Vivien Leigh production of *Romeo and Juliet* foundered on precisely the same shoal, and it was not until the completely automated décor for *Oliver* in 1960 that the idea was got absolutely right.) The play opened what was supposed to be its pre-New York try-out tour in Boston in February 1939, staggered on in a similarly chaotic state, with cuts and additions bedevilling the poor actors almost every night and the Theatre Guild snapping at its heels over the rapidly escalating budget, to Washington and then to Philadelphia, where the Guild finally withdrew its support. Frantic attempts by Welles to raise the necessary extra money on the security of his own inheritance, which he would not come into until he was twenty-five in a few months' time, had no result, and Welles sadly called it a day, putting the sets and costumes of *Five Kings* in storage in New York until more favourable times should come.

With Hollywood even more enthusiastically after him since the *War of the Worlds* sensation (if he could do it once, he could do it again) and since his tantalizingly inconclusive experience filming the prologue for *Too Much Johnson*, the films looked like an even more attractive option. But before he plumped definitely for the West Coast, he had one more characteristically eccentric stab at the live theatre. In the heyday of vaudeville some of the biggest serious stars, like Bernhardt and Pavlova, had toured with it (Bernhardt once, unthinkably, played on the same bill with Mae West), so why should not the boy wonder do likewise? He retained fond memories of the vaudevillians who stayed at his father's hotel in his childhood, and a life-long respect for vaudeville skills. Nothing loath, once he had conceived the idea, he concocted for himself a twenty-minute précis of William Archer's reliable melodrama *The Green Goddess*, already used on his radio drama series, in which he would play the Rajah of Rook as various great stars of the day might have played him, thereby utilizing his famous gifts of mimicry. Unfortunately, the vaudeville circuit and its audiences were not what they had been – or maybe Welles was just not what they wanted. The act laid an egg, and after some weeks of empty houses he gave up for good.

But there was always this sudden, surprising display of interest on the part of George J. Schaefer, brand-new president in charge of production at RKO-Radio. They wanted him to act, but also to direct. Going by his usual schedule for stage work, that should not be too difficult or take too long. Probably he could make a film in six months or so, repair his shattered finances, then return to New York and *Five Kings*. Or so he may have thought. On the other hand, if he had really got the film-making bug already, this looked like a good chance to find out. At least he could go out himself and explore the possibilities. On 20 June 1939 he arrived in Los Angeles, checked into the Chateau Marmont, took a deep breath and looked around.

Shooting
for the
Moon

3

IF HE HAD DONE IT ONCE, HE COULD DO IT AGAIN . . . It is important in looking at Welles's arrival in Hollywood and the extraordinary contract his agent Arnold Weissburger managed to get out of RKO to be quite clear what the 'it' was. What Welles had done was to hit the headlines with amazing consistency for someone with such lofty ambitions. The 'panic broadcast' had been only the most spectacular instance. But, right from the black *Macbeth* onwards, Welles had shown an uncanny knack, not only of delivering enough quality to keep the intellectual audiences agog, but also of doing it in the most public and newsworthy way, so that he was a name and had achieved a notoriety even with millions who had never had the chance to sample most of his work. That talent was worth gambling a bit of money on, even in Hollywood.

And that sort of gamble is just what Schaefer and RKO decided to take. The very nature of Welles's contract, which tied him to make two films, the first by New Year 1940, the second by New Year 1941 (getting paid $100,000 for the first and $125,000 for the second, plus percentages of the profits after RKO had made back their initial envisaged outlay of $500,000 per picture), both of which Welles would produce, direct, write and appear in, was news in itself, all going cleverly to support Welles's public image of the wonder boy, the mad, untamable genius who might take over the world. If we look more closely we can see that RKO were not risking that much: with their million-dollar investment they were buying a million dollars' worth of publicity, plus two pictures that might or might not succeed. And all Welles's much-vaunted total control over the pictures from inception to release was limited by the studio's absolute right to reject a project if they cared to, plus all sorts of get-outs in the small print if the mercurial Welles did not live up to his side of the bargain.

Even so, there is no particular reason to be too cynical about Schaefer's motives. No doubt he did genuinely want to restore a bit of class to RKO's act, and Welles seemed like a perfectly likely way of doing it. Indeed, as long as Schaefer was in charge Welles was left remarkably undisturbed. The trouble was that RKO had been throughout its career worryingly changeable at the top, and Schaefer was not going to remain in charge for more than three years. After which . . . well, after which many of the resentments which had been buzzing around in Hollywood over the very idea of giving this pretentious, know-nothing kid from the New York theatre a virtual carte blanche which even highly experienced film-makers could not command, came home to roost. As Welles himself later remarked, 'I would have hated myself too,' adding: 'Of course the producers hated me most because if I could do all those things, what was the need of a producer?' Certainly, a lot of people in Hollywood longed to see Welles fall flat on his face, and were going to do their utmost to make sure that he did.

For the moment, however, the first question, after Welles had settled into a palatial home a stone's-throw from Shirley Temple and effectively parried questions from the Press about his ailing marriage, was what would the first project be? Welles's own favourite seems to have been Conrad's short novel *The Heart of Darkness* (eventually to be filmed in almost equally dramatic circumstances by Francis Ford Coppola as *Apocalypse Now*). He had already adapted it for radio, and was much taken with the idea of playing both the invisible narrator Marlow, who represents the audience's eye in the film, and his legendary quarry and in a sense his doppelgänger Kurtz, the man who rules the African natives right in the heart of the darkness at the end of Marlow's quest. He wrote a script which failed to find favour with the studio, but he was working simultaneously on at least two other ideas: a mainly comic adaptation of the Nicholas Blake (the pen-name of C. Day Lewis) thriller novel *The Smiler with a Knife*, to star possibly Carole Lombard or Lucille Ball, and a Mexican melodrama of his own, loosely based on

41

Arthur Calder-Marshall's novel *The Way to Santiago*, which as envisaged by Welles came to look more and more like a more accessible reworking of *The Heart of Darkness* idea. At one point Welles was so keen to make *The Heart of Darkness* that he even offered to throw in *The Smiler with a Knife* free if RKO would let him. But even on those terms, nothing came of the notion.

This had something to do with the increasing complexity of Welles's situation – from 10 September he had to fly to New York and back once a week to keep up his radio commitments – and something to do with the gathering storm clouds in Europe, where Germany had invaded Poland in September, thereby starting the Second World War. Though the States were not directly involved as yet, the war meant that Welles could not get the female star he wanted for *The Heart of Darkness*, Dita Parlo, as she was interned in Austria, and, more significantly, it cut out almost completely the sophisticated European market for Hollywood's 'quality' products, which had supplied most of the profits for such as Garbo's last half-dozen pictures. It was more important than ever that Welles should not only bring in the publicity (which he automatically continued to do) but also deliver a not-too-expensive film which could be a popular hit in the home market.

The first realistic budget for *The Heart of Darkness*, prepared when Welles was already rehearsing his actors in November, turned out to be more than a million dollars, or twice the previously agreed amount. Even so, Schaefer did not yet definitively say no, but as there was no hope of Welles delivering a picture by the 1 January deadline stipulated in his contract, he had to do some quick thinking. Especially since he had managed to get the Campbell Playhouse radio shows shifted to Los Angeles and subsidized them by casting a lot of his old Mercury Theatre players in *The Heart of Darkness*, thereby getting them on the RKO payroll. When *The Heart of Darkness* was put off until

at least March, they were immediately dropped, and one motive for pushing *The Smiler with a Knife*, even to promising to add it free of extra charge to his contract, was to get them back on again.

By the end of the year Welles had also agreed with Virginia to end their marriage with a formal separation, followed by a divorce the next February, and quarrelled with John Houseman, who had been working with him in New York and on the coast with all his film, radio and theatre projects. What he desperately needed now was a real film to make. Some time in February he decided he had got just what he needed, threw all other ideas aside, and got down to work on the idea which was to become *Citizen Kane*. To help him with it he rehired Houseman, and enlisted Herman J. Mankiewicz, successful screen-writer, drunk, brother of Joseph L., and, more immediately, a regular writer for the Welles radio shows and collaborator on *The Smiler with a Knife* script. Thus began a saga of argument and ill-will. In the *New Yorker* article which eventually became the main text of her *Citizen Kane Book*, Pauline Kael argued in 1971 that Welles, as was his wont, had hogged all the credit for something that was basically not his: the whole conception of *Citizen Kane*, story and structure, was, she argued, Mankiewicz's, and adduced various parallels from his earlier scripting work to prove it. This is the old argument about the importance of Welles's collaborators in his theatre work, more forcefully re-stated. And no one in his right mind (including even Orson Welles) would deny that Mankiewicz must have made a very important contribution to the elaboration of *Citizen Kane*, especially in terms of technical know-how. But Roger Carringer's painstaking step-by-step analysis of the various drafts of the *Kane* script and the process of actually shooting seems to dispose conclusively of any notion that Mankiewicz was largely or wholly responsible for the script and Welles just a flashy opportunist, ready himself or urged by the studio to grab all the

Welles on the camera boom, in his costume and makeup as the middle-aged Kane, directing *Citizen Kane*. Below: (top) as Kane utters the famous last word, 'Rosebud', the miniature snow-storm in a glass globe falls from his hand. (Bottom) Young Kane is playing in the snow with his sledge Rosebud when he is taken away from home.

credit because it aggrandized him and made a better story.

Apart from anything else, there are very clear autobiographical connotations in Welles's picture of Charles Foster Kane, demonically driven tycoon and demagogue, though audiences at the time were hardly in a position to know that. The most obvious is the naming of young Kane's kindly, protective guardian as Bernstein, like Welles's own. Another is the depiction of Kane's longtime friend and drama critic on his newspaper, Leland, which is unmistakably based on Ashton Stevens, friend of the Welles family, early supporter of Welles himself, and drama critic on the *Chicago American*, a paper owned and run by the almighty William Randolph Hearst. For Hearst was undoubtedly, whatever Welles might say then or subsequently, the principal model for Kane himself. There may even have been a deliberate touch of revenge in the portrayal, since Hearst papers had lately been saying some very damning things about Welles's theatre work (a Hearst critic described *Horse Eats Hat* as 'an outmoded farce ... garnished with sewage'), and Welles's wide-eyed assertions that Kane was drawn from many sources, including the other Chicago millionaire Samuel Insull, who built the opera house primarily, it was alleged, as a showcase for his own would-be opera-singer love, just as Kane promoted the hopeless career of Susan Alexander, were clearly as disingenuous as they seemed.

But whatever the Hearst press thought about *Citizen Kane* when it finally emerged, there seems no doubt that its most important motive was to invent a compelling story with a fascinating and mysterious central character for Welles to play: the sources of the material in real life were haphazard and coincidental. The script which emerged from the February-to-June to-and-fro between Welles and Mankiewicz – Welles providing the outlines, Mankiewicz fleshing out the scenes, Welles rewriting Mankiewicz, Mankiewicz rewriting

Welles shows us Kane first as a clear-eyed young man
(note the 'k' on the collar), then with the added maturity
implied by a moustache.

Welles's rewrites – was a very direct expression of Welles's need to do something and a crystallization of a number of ideas about dramatic character and structure that he had been playing around with for several years – most recently in the quest-structure of *The Heart of Darkness*. By June the script was almost finalized, and Welles was ready to start shooting, with his cast all assembled, drawn mainly from the ranks of his Mercury familiars on stage and radio, with only the two female romantic leads, Ruth Warrick as Kane's starchy wife and Dorothy Comingore as his pretty, pathetic mistress, from outside the charmed circle. Fearing studio interference – RKO was pressing him to follow up his 'panic broadcast' reputation by making something called *The Men from Mars* – he hit on the ruse, not dissimilar from the way Alfred Hitchcock got to make his first talkie, *Blackmail*, without his studio realizing the fact till too late, of making an extensive series of 'tests' which only later proved to be part of the film proper.

The official shooting began on 29 June, and finished on 23 October 1940. Under four months now seems very modest, especially for a film of such complexity, but at the time it was quite long enough to give further colour to partly studio-inspired tales of Welles's extravagance and perfectionism, à la 'the man you loved to hate' Erich von Stroheim, whose follies and fantasies as a director were not yet forgotten in Hollywood and provided a convenient publicity-model for the workings of a mad genius. In fact, all things considered (including that this was, after all, his first feature film in any capacity, let alone all), Welles worked with remarkable economy and precision, carefully rehearsing his cast to get exactly the effect he wanted before shooting a foot of film on each scene. There are many witnesses to the frenzy and single-mindedness with which he worked a sixteen- or even eighteen-hour day, and despite covert attempts on the part of the studio to find out just what was going on – understandable enough, if contrary to the

letter of his contract – and other temporary foul-ups which a paranoically-inclined Welles was quite capable of exaggerating into a campaign against him, the shooting was completed only about three weeks behind schedule and not too drastically over budget. As he settled down to the task of editing his material – something which was already done in large measure in his head – Welles had good reason to be satisfied with his work. Though even he at that time could hardly have suspected how good was his reason – or that it would dog him for the rest of his life. As he said later when working on *F for Fake* in 1973: 'I began at the top and have been making my way down ever since.'

Even before the picture was completed, there was trouble and to spare. In an outburst of folly they were rapidly to regret, Mercury Productions, Welles's own production company, arranged for a 'secret' advance screening to select magazine critics while such details as Bernard Herrmann's vitally important music track had yet to be added – and omitted to invite either of Hollywood's unofficial arbiters, Hedda Hopper and Louella Parsons. Hedda heard about it, insisted on attending, and then wrote a savage attack on Welles for his 'vicious and irresponsible' depiction of Hearst, for whom she did not even work. To make matters worse, Louella, who did, had always appeared to be a supporter of Welles, but now found that as well as not having seen the film when it seemed everyone else had, she was made fun of in a newspaper quote which had Welles explicitly stating that the film was 'about her boss'. Welles very likely did say something of the sort – like Oscar Wilde, he was inclined to let his tongue run away with him at just the moments when he should most firmly have held it in check – but now all his denials and apologies could make no difference: the full force of the vast Hearst Press empire was brought to bear to see that, if at all possible, the film should not be shown and he never work again.

[CONT'D PAGE 53]

47

Kane and his longtime friend and drama critic Leland
(Welles and Joseph Cotten) stand triumphantly in the
middle of Kane's paper empire. Below: even Citizen Kane
started small – Cotten, Welles and Everett Sloane in the
office of his first publishing venture.

Kane's stag dinner for his old associate Bernstein (Everett Sloane) includes the inevitable ingredient of showgirls for tired businessmen. Welles, of course, was on hand, both as actor and directing the intricately conceived sequence.

The women in Kane's life, wife (Ruth Warrick) and
mistress (Dorothy Comingore). Neither has a very good
time: the mistress is finally reduced to playing endlessly
with jigsaw puzzles amid the monumental decors of Kane's
castle, Xanadu.

The woman in Welles's life at this time: maturely beautiful Mexican star Dolores del Rio, from whom he was inseparable for a couple of years.

Fortunately, whatever blackmail Hearst might try to exert behind the scenes, he had no leg to stand on in public, because the thing he most resented about the film – its apparent references to his long-standing relationship with the film star Marion Davies – was just what he least wanted aired and dragged through the courts. Everyone knew, of course, but nobody said, and how dare this egotistic young pup break the conspiracy of silence – especially since his ex-wife had just married Marion Davies's favourite nephew Charles Lederer, so it was almost like betrayal within the family? Even so, a libel action was always a possibility, so to anticipate such a problem (or anticipate RKO shareholders' anticipating such a problem) Welles threatened to file a suit against RKO if it did not, as contracted, release the film. Meanwhile, he went to New York with his newest love, Mexican film star Dolores Del Rio, to direct Richard Wright's powerful drama on a racial theme (adapted for the stage in collaboration with Paul Green) *Native Son*, which was produced by John Houseman.

The play got notices ranging from the enthusiastic ('By all odds the strongest drama of the season,' said *Time* magazine) to the savagely dismissive. These were mostly on account of its evident leftist sympathies, which gave Hearst's *Journal American* a chance to label it and its director Communist. Though the apolitical Welles had come in his Mercury Theatre years to realize the advantages, in New York at least, of a certain amount of fashionable fellow-travelling to ensure a faithful left-wing audience, the charge could as far as he was concerned hardly be wider of the mark: a determined individualist and Nietzschean from his youth, it would have made more sense to label him a fascist by temperament and an artist by conviction, and leave it at that. However, the Hearst Press was quite favourable towards European fascists, and 'artist', however dirty a word, did not seem a big enough stick with which to beat the maker of *Citizen Kane*, so 'Communist' had to do.

For all Welles's fears, *Citizen Kane* opened spectacularly enough in New York on 1 May 1941, at the Palace Theatre in default of the 'unavailable' Radio City Music Hall, and received notices of an ecstatic enthusiasm it would be hard to equal – except of course from the Hearst publications, which would not even accept advertisements for it. Ironically, it seems likely that the good reviews did the picture more harm than all Hearst's opposition: while that at least made *Kane* sound controversial and scandalous, and no doubt entertaining, the critics made it sound high-brow and cultural and difficult, which was much more like a kiss of death: entertainment-hungry audiences were hardly likely to be enthusiastic about 'important new techniques in picture-making and story-telling' (*Time*) or 'Such original techniques, such exciting photography' (*Life*). Nor should we let Welles's conspiracy theory, reasonable enough in itself (after all, he was being conspired against), make us forget how difficult the film in fact was to ordinary non-specialized audiences at that time, and what poor word-of-mouth publicity it was likely to get. If *Danton's Death* could fail abysmally without the might of Hearst ranged against it, and that in the much more specialized field of New York advanced theatre, why should not *Kane*, for all its later reputation, have an even more acute problem getting the mass audience it needed for immediate success, into the cinema?

Citizen Kane was then, and is now, essentially a film-maker's film. Welles had learnt his lessons well, in a crash course which encompassed everything from *The Cabinet of Doctor Caligari* to *Stagecoach*, and had made the fullest possible use of the artist-technicians on his team, their skills and their eagerness, for once, to experiment. The successful cameraman Gregg Toland actually came and asked to work for him, and told Welles: 'There's nothing I couldn't teach you in three hours.'

There was possibly nothing in the film that was absolutely unprecedented – everything

that struck contemporary viewers as so extraordinary, like Toland's deep-focus photography, that kept foreground and background in sharp focus at the same time, or Percy Ferguson's elaborate period sets *with ceilings*, so as to permit very low-angle shots, or Robert Wise's bold editorial transitions from scene to scene, as in the famous sequence in which Kane's marriage is encapsulated in three continuous breakfast scenes spread over several years, or the whole fragmented structure of Mankiewicz's and Welles's script, could certainly be found somewhere else, some time earlier, in at least an embryonic form. What was original was the continuous barrage of such effects, forging a highly personal film language of quite baroque intricacy and splendour, and the confident showmanship with which they were presented to the public. And those belonged to Welles alone.

It is perfectly understandable that *Citizen Kane* should have had such an overwhelming influence on Hollywood films that came after.

Shaw remarked of Ibsen's impact on late nineteenth-century England, 'A modern manager need not produce *The Wild Duck*, but he must be very careful not to produce a play which will seem insipid and old-fashioned to play-goers who have seen *The Wild Duck*, even though they may have hissed it.' The same exactly was true of Welles and *Kane* in the Hollywood of the 1940s. But on the whole each film-maker who felt the influence took one or two devices from the film; none dared to run the risk of overloading that Welles cheerfully shouldered, that indeed he could do nothing without. The film, it has been complained, is nothing but a bag of tricks. Fair enough, in a way: but what else would one expect of a young man in a hurry, his head full of possibilities, who is suddenly handed what he once called 'the best goddamned box of toys any boy ever had'? All Welles's multitudinous and sometimes unruly talents are on view in *Citizen Kane*. But it left one big question unanswered: now that he had shown he had them, how con-

vincingly could he show that he knew how best to use them? That, as he must have realized himself, was what his second film must be all about.

Clearly, as long as George Schaefer was in charge at RKO, there was going to be a second film, even though the returns for the first film were so disappointing, and after its first runs the exposure it received was minimal. But for all their sakes he had to move with unaccustomed caution, and make no false moves. Clearly the idea he had toyed with of a film on the life of Christ, with himself as Jesus, was out. So was his fantasy of adapting *The Pickwick Papers*, which he had already done on The Mercury Theatre on the Air, only this time with W. C. Fields, since Fields was by now almost as risky a proposition as he was himself. There was always his 'Mexican melodrama', which was now especially attractive to him as a vehicle for Dolores Del Rio, but it proved a lot less attractive to the Mexican government, on account of a certain political sensitiveness,

so that was not too viable. He fancied *Cyrano de Bergerac* as a vehicle for himself, but the public, when polled, showed a monumental lack of interest. Then he fancied directing Charles Chaplin in his own fictionalized version of the Landru wife-murders, but Chaplin did not want to be directed by anyone but himself, so bought from Welles the outline which eventually became *Monsieur Verdoux*.

Baulked of all these possibilities, he came round to what his advisers were always urging on him: a couple of relatively straightforward adaptations, one of Eric Ambler's thriller *Journey into Fear*, which he would produce and star in (with Dolores Del Rio), but not direct, and the other – for the second he hit upon Booth Tarkington's novel *The Magnificent Ambersons*, which again had autobiographical resonances for him (Tarkington was a close friend of his father's) and which also he had already adapted for radio, himself playing the spoilt son and heir George, who eventually gets his come-uppance. He felt he was too old and

too overweight to play the role on screen, but then he did not have to, as his old contract had been scrapped and a new, less advantageous one substituted, in which for the two remaining films he had agreed to make he was not required to appear himself, or direct, but merely produce, and did not have a right to the final cut.

Since his financial position was urgently in need of repair, Welles took up again a heavy schedule of radio shows and occasional, rather fanciful (and maybe apocryphal) vaudeville appearances as an illusionist. By October he had finished the script for *Ambersons*, and was ready to begin shooting, almost exactly a year after he had completed shooting on *Citizen Kane*. Like *Citizen Kane*, the film was all subject to detailed rehearsal in advance, and was

all shot in about the same length of time, from 28 October 1941 to 31 January 1942. And this even though Welles was also occupied with the Lady Esther Face Powder radio show, was scripting *Journey into Fear* in collaboration with *Magnificent Ambersons* leading man Joseph Cotten, and was already supervising at a distance second-unit shooting on yet another project, an episode film to be called *It's All True* which would take in a potted history of jazz with Duke Ellington, a visit to the carnival in Rio, and a touching story by Robert Flaherty of a friendship between a boy and a bull, location material for which was already being shot in Mexico by former actor Norman Foster.

Opinions differed over whether Welles was again pushing himself too hard, spreading himself too thin, or whether he had to work in this

The Magnificent Ambersons. **Opposite: the product of them, Aunt Fanny (Agnes Moorehead) and young George (Tim Holt) riding for a fall in the midst of their ornate mansion. Below: Welles plans his camera movements on the set-designer's model for the Amberson home.**

sort of frenzy because he knew no other way. Whatever the answer, it did not seem to damage his work on *The Magnificent Ambersons*: since the narrative was more straightforward than in *Kane*, much less fragmented, he was able to call forth something more recognizable as independent performances from his cast (perhaps especially since this time he was not, much to his relief he claimed, one of them). He assumed, with the aid of his new cameraman Stanley Cortez, an equally richly textured but much more consistent visual style, depending sometimes, as in the opening ball scene, on intricate moving-camera shots but sometimes, as in the famous scene where the insufferable George (Tim Holt) taunts his neurotic maiden aunt (Agnes Moorehead) over some strawberry shortcake, leaving the camera just where it was throughout a whole sustained scene. (Each solution was of course equally unorthodox in relation to the 'normal' Hollywood studio style of matching cross-cut close-ups framed by medium shots and establishing long shots.) The most ambitious aspect of the film was Welles's bold idea of parallelling the fall of the magnificent Ambersons' family fortunes with monumental, almost documentary, sequences showing the changes overtaking the Mid-Western community all round them. The film, in all its planned elaboration, was more than half shot when Japan attacked Pearl Harbor on 7 December and at last America entered the Second World War.

This apparent irrelevance to an elaborate period-piece being shot on a sound stage in Hollywood was not in fact as irrelevant as it

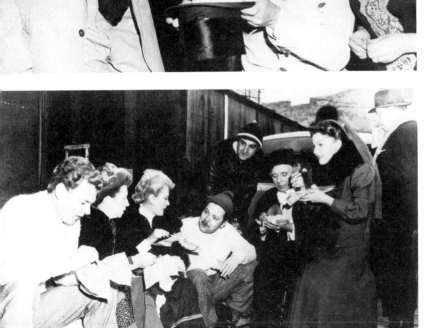

seemed. Though Welles was theoretically of call-up age, it was unlikely, given his weight problem, his chronic asthma and his damaged back, the legacy of an early childhood condition, that he actually would be conscripted. However, a more or less chance meeting with Nelson Rockefeller, who had recently been put in charge by Roosevelt of 'Inter-American Affairs' (which meant the Good Neighbour policy and keeping Latin American sympathies on the right side), made a crucial and in the end a disastrous difference to Welles – all in the cause of the new war effort. The episode film *It's All True*, which Welles was already in a desultory way working on, happened to chime very well with Rockefeller's Pan-American initiative, and since Rockefeller also happened to be a major shareholder in RKO, nothing appeared more logical than that the government should put some money into the project and it should be moved to first priority after *The Magnificent Ambersons* – the more so since the Rio Mardi Gras carnival, which everyone agreed would be perfect for an elaborate colour sequence, was coming up quite early in the New Year. Welles agreed to the idea, and stepped up shooting on *The*

61

Magnificent Ambersons so that he could be finished in time to fly to Rio, and come back to edit *Ambersons* later. It would be not only a golden opportunity, but his patriotic duty as well. And that way he might escape tactfully from Dolores Del Rio, with whom his affair was cooling as her divorce and their planned marriage approached.

It was at this point that things began to go badly wrong. Even though Welles did not have any more the contractual right to final cut on his second feature, if he was around he would probably be able to push through its completion very much the way he wanted it. On the other hand, if he was in another hemisphere it was doubtful whether those he left behind to prepare the rough cut according to his instructions, a faithful team headed by Robert Wise, would have sufficient clout to withstand studio interference, should any materialize – and with the number of enemies Welles had made at RKO it almost certainly would. And then, to add unnecessarily to his already heavy load of troubles, he had resolved to put *Journey into Fear* into production in his absence, under the direction of Norman Foster, appointed on the strength of his work on the still uncompleted Mexican episode of *It's All True*. Welles's own role in the thriller, as a villainous Turkish police chief, was episodic and could, he decided, be all shot before he went to Brazil. He would have nothing to do with the direction – well, a little *advice* possibly, but it would mostly be done in his absence. During January 1942 he was directing two parallel units on *Ambersons*, to speed things up, shooting his role in *Journey into Fear* at night ('My very hammy performance. It was *meant* to be a hammy performance'), and somehow finding time for Lady Esther too. At last on 2 February he completed his work on *Journey into Fear*, and was able to get off to Rio, cramming in an intensive three-day session on the first cut of *Ambersons* with Robert Wise in Miami before departure. Against all odds, everything seemed to be working out all right . . .

That may have been Welles's impression, as he joined enthusiastically in the Rio revels, shot miles of film with a 16 mm camera and tried to work out what he was going to do with it. But it was far from the truth. Wise was supposed to fly down to Rio on 1 March with the reels of the edited *Ambersons*, for more work on the fine tuning. Unfortunately, before that could happen, civilians had been forbidden to fly abroad, and so the film was dispatched to Rio without Wise on 11 March, not to arrive in Welles's hands for several weeks. And meanwhile a sneak preview of the rough cut had been arranged in the Los Angeles suburb of Pomona for 17 March. It happened, and it was by all accounts a total disaster. The sort of disaster neither Schaefer nor RKO could afford. And Welles was far away, impossible even to talk to. So, sadly, the inevitable happened: the studio insisted that the film be cut and reshot in order to make it acceptable to a popular audience. And the Welles team, including such personal friends as Joseph Cotten and Robert Wise, actually connived at this massacre of his masterpiece. Or that was the way that Welles regarded their actions when he heard. Of course, they were in an impossible position back in Hollywood. No doubt they all thought they were acting in the best interests of the film, the company and Welles himself to salvage what they could – even if it meant reducing the film from 131 minutes to 88, removing most of Welles's historical-documentary framework in favour of the plot (though Welles afterwards said that the framework *was* the plot, the montage sequences showing the history of the town in counterpoint to that of the family being 'the whole heart of the picture, really'), and reworking the ending to make it lighter and more palatable.

Naturally, Welles regarded it all as yet another, more total betrayal. But then he angrily rejected the slightest suggestion there could have been anything wrong with his version, and it is difficult to wonder if he was right, or whether – perish the thought – the new,

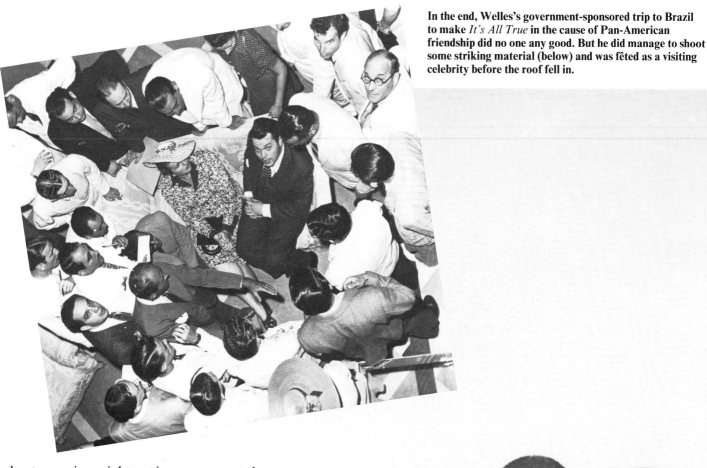

In the end, Welles's government-sponsored trip to Brazil to make *It's All True* in the cause of Pan-American friendship did no one any good. But he did manage to shoot some striking material (below) and was fêted as a visiting celebrity before the roof fell in.

shorter version might not in some respects have been an improvement. Certainly the film as it exists today is in most respects so wonderful, so mature, so coherent, and (many feel) superior to *Citizen Kane* that one must at least agree with Robert Wise that whatever he and his fellows may have done to the picture, 'since *Ambersons* has become something of a classic, I think it's now apparent we didn't mutilate Orson's film.' And all this while they were still, many of them, struggling on with *Journey into Fear* and their leader, incommunicado, was having the time of his life in Brazil.

For undoubtedly, until the bad news started to filter through, Welles was really enjoying himself. Admittedly, he did get himself shot at from time to time (or so he claimed) by jealous husbands and lovers, but he loved the colour and life of Rio, and he had soon worked out what the major episode of *It's All True* was going to be about: it was going to synthesize the carnival material into a history of the

samba (replacing, presumably, the earlier-planned history of jazz), and cross-cut that with the heroic story, currently topical in Brazil, of four jangadeiros (river fishermen) who had come 1,650 miles down the Amazon by raft in order to lodge a protest about their terrible living conditions. Or possibly there would be two separate episodes, depending on whether Welles could conjure up enough money to shoot them both in colour. He continued shooting material and living it up in Rio until early June, despite the unfortunate drowning of one of the original jangadeiros in an accident while he was restaging their triumphant arrival in Rio harbour. Most of the unit returned to the States on 8 June, but Welles stayed on for a further six weeks with a skeleton crew to shoot footage necessary for the start of the jangadeiros episode in their distant home town of Fortazela.

It was here that, early in July, he heard the news: Schaefer, his only hope at RKO, had been ousted; the contract with Mercury Productions had been instantly cancelled, and *Journey into Fear* confiscated for recutting by the new studio bosses; and the premiere of *The Magnificent Ambersons* had been set for 13 August, much too soon for him to do anything to restore it even had he possessed the power to insist on doing so. Still, he reasoned, something could probably be salvaged: at least with government backing (no one told him it had already been effectively withdrawn) he should be able to complete *It's All True* when he got back to the States. After all, that was not controversial or difficult in any way; just a straightforward entertainment film designed in a non-doctrinaire way to cement Pan-American friendship. When he set off from Rio on 29 July he did not even hurry home, but stopped off in several capitals en route, including an unexpectedly loving reunion in Mexico City with his now ex-fiancée Dolores Del Rio. Even when he got home, he did not fully realize the harm the Brazilian adventure had done his career, and just how far out in the cold he now was.

Orson Welles

*The boy
from Brazil
and the
lady from
Shanghai*

4

AT FIRST THE LET-DOWN WAS GRADUAL. THE NEW men at RKO were willing to talk – if only because they realized that only Welles could make anything out of the Brazilian material, and in any case if he contractually owed them another film, they in their turn owed him the chance to make it, or get paid for not making it. Also, they had botched *Journey into Fear* and badly needed him to re-edit and re-shoot it into showable form – which, rather surprisingly, he agreed to do with Joseph Cotten for expenses only: perhaps they felt that since their names were all over it, they had better do something for their own protection. But it soon became clear to Welles, even in his moments of wildest optimism, that RKO was not going to let him make a third film, and if anything was to be done with *It's All True* it would be entirely up to him to do it – at his own expense if necessary. He managed to get RKO to release the material, developed and undeveloped, to him, and started to work on it independently. He could keep himself on his radio work, which still continued to be plentiful. But to get anywhere with *It's All True* he needed a lot more money than he earned from that. The only way to get it was to star in somebody else's film.

In later years this was Welles's normal way of financing his own creative ventures, and even then, when he was a very well-known actor much in demand, it seldom worked out very well – hence, he insisted, his long string of unfinished films and unrealized projects. But in Hollywood in 1942, at the height of the studio-factory system, it was a very eccentric way indeed of proceeding. Fortunately, he received a timely offer. Selznick was setting up a film version of *Jane Eyre*, another classic property Welles had adapted and starred in for radio. He had his director, a promising young British émigré and conscientious objector called Robert Stevenson, and Joan Fontaine, fresh from winning her Oscar for *Suspicion*, was to play Jane. But Selznick was desperate to find an appropriate Rochester, and it was a part that Welles, with his imperious manner

and his wild romantic eyes, seemed born to play – provided, of course, he could slim down for it. Welles anticipated no great problem there, and when the call came from Selznick he was ready. A contract to star and function as associate producer for $100,000 was the result, which held good even when Selznick sold the whole package to Twentieth Century Fox. Welles's only special condition was that he should be given editing facilities and be able to continue with *It's All True* in his own time.

It may have been all true, but it wasn't all there. That was the painful bottom line to Welles's six wasted months in Brazil. Though some of the carnival material is alleged by those who saw it at the time to be remarkable – nowadays, when the background is so much more familiar and colour coverage a staple of everyday television, the few unearthed fragments look fairly ordinary – Welles did not have enough material in the can to make into a coherent film, even a shortish one, without prohibitively expensive extra shooting, which could not but look to such as Zanuck and Selznick like pouring good money after bad. Gradually Welles's hopes of making anything of it receded, though every now and then, even twenty-five years later, he would bring up the possibility of resurrecting the idea and maybe selling it to television.

And already he was getting into his role in *Jane Eyre*. This was to relaunch his career as a star actor. And it was a role that, despite his protestations, he seemed rather to enjoy. That was just in front of the camera. Behind the camera was another and more contentious matter. When Welles was accused in later years of taking an uncredited hand in the direction of any or all of his films as an actor, he would generally vociferously deny it, and then, if there was any credit to be gained from the added involvement, whimsically half take his denial back. Of *The Third Man*, for instance, which has been seen by some as the most Wellesian of all the films he didn't direct, he insisted firmly that he did not direct a frame of it, and then added cryptically, 'But of course I was

Periodically, Welles had a fancy to play the romantic leading man, and the brooding Mr Rochester in *Jane Eyre* was a role made-to-measure. Joan Fontaine was the timid governess he fascinates and terrifies.

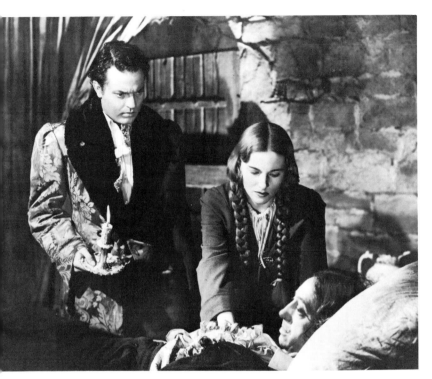

there all the time.' In any case, *Jane Eyre* was the first film in which, though he received only an acting credit (even the associate producer credit was finally withdrawn), rumour had it he played an important role in 'directing the director on how to direct'. Maybe he did, maybe he didn't – as usual, he always explicitly denied everything. But there is no doubt that at least he directed his own acting part, and probably proffered a hint here and there elsewhere, as an associate producer legitimately might. And whatever the truth of the matter, he turned in one of his most effective screen performances, and in consequence found a whole new type of career opening out for him.

Not, probably, that it was or could ever have been enough. Not even his burgeoning relationship with the new love of his life, Rita Hayworth, already marked in his mind to be the second Mrs Orson Welles, could wholly replace the terrible urge to create, and the need

to assuage wounded pride by making a new masterpiece to blot out previous defeats. The 'second Mrs Orson Welles' was, like Dolores Del Rio, someone he had been first violently attracted to on the screen, some time before he ever met her. (It was one of the advantages of being a Hollywood *wunderkind* that you could quite possibly make such teenage dreams reality.) He had first been excited by Dolores Del Rio, according to his own account, when he saw her swimming as near naked as was then allowed in some silent South Seas epic when he was eleven. (He was very likely overestimating his precocity – if that were possible – and ungallantly overestimating the lady's age: he was almost certainly thinking of Vidor's talkie *Bird of Paradise*, which came out when he was eighteen.) Rita Hayworth was an idol of his rather more mature years, and did not have quite such a traumatic original impact on him; it does not seem to be recorded in what movie he first noticed her – might it have been *Blood and Sand* in 1941? – but since she was *the* big new star sensation of the years when Welles first arrived in Hollywood, it would have been difficult for him to remain unaware of her. And, like Dolores Del Rio, she came from a Latin background (Welles for some reason always wanted to believe that it was gypsy rather than Spanish) which had been very important in her teens when she spent a lot of time in Mexico partnering her father in a Spanish dance act – though by the time she became a big star her dark hair had been dyed red and she came over as the athletic all-American girl. Spanish dancer or all-American, Welles did not care: he was determined to meet and win her.

He did actually manage to set up a casual-seeming meeting while he was making *Jane Eyre*. There was an immediate rapport with Rita, who was three years younger than he but a longer-established movie star, having played her first major role in *Only Angels Have Wings* in 1939. The meeting must have been rather like the later, classic encounter between Marilyn

69

Monroe and Arthur Miller: the sex goddess meets the great intellectual, and sparks fly. For Rita, like Marilyn, was as gorgeous physically off screen as on, but otherwise dreadfully self-conscious about her lack of education and emotionally very insecure. Welles, with all his bounding self-confidence and his reputation as an all-purpose mastermind, was just the sort of man she could look up to and depend on – and he had the advantage of being very sexy into the bargain. Welles soon found the frightened little girl hidden inside the mature and splendid woman, and reacted to it with unaccustomed gentleness: he was delighted to be mentor and guide to one of the most beautiful and desired women in the world.

But while the relationship developed, he needed, as usual, to be busy at other things. At this middle period of the war there was, for the first time in his life, not really enough for him to do, not to keep his boundless energy more than half occupied. There was radio, a lot of which now became a sort of war-work, making informative and patriotic addresses to the troops and those at home. There was politics, of a sort, for though Welles had never

taken too much interest in anything outside showbusiness, he presciently divined that a lot of politics was even then, long before the days of television debates and film-star presidents, just an extension of show-business. Welles was always an eloquent public speaker, especially if well briefed, and in his period of relative inactivity he toyed for a while with political ambitions, intervening in specific questions about which he knew something, like the status of Mexican immigrants in the States, and, under the influence of a rather mysterious figure, international financier and political propagandist Louis Dolivet, in matters about which he knew nothing but with which he could, like Charles Foster Kane, make a good showing on a platform.

But though he played politics for a while, his heart was not really in it. Much more to his taste, in fact, allowing him to display all his extrovert nature, was the work he did to entertain the troops, particularly in the *Mercury Wonder Show*, a tent-show he put on in Los Angeles and then on tour, which featured (of course) his magician act and used a number of Mercury regulars like Joseph Cotten and Agnes Moorehead in highly unlikely ways – Cotten as an escapologist, Moorehead minced up, only to reappear whole at the end of the scene. The climax of the show was supposed to be Welles cutting Rita in half, but before too long Harry Cohn, her boss at Columbia, said a very definite no (maybe jealous or maybe just mistrusting Welles's skills with a saw), and so Marlene Dietrich took her place in the act. This is the only one of Welles's more fantastic theatrical excursions that has been adequately preserved for us: in 1944 he recreated the turn with Marlene Dietrich for insertion in Eddie Sutherland's slapdash film review *Follow the Boys*.

In more general terms, though, offers were not exactly pouring in. Though he kept on agitating the fragments of *It's All True* in the waters, the fish were still not biting; and though *Jane Eyre* had a significant success, no one was

**Something for the troops: Welles's *Mercury Wonder
Show*, played in tents for the benefit of the services, with
Joseph Cotten and Rita Hayworth participating. Below:
the filmed excerpt in *Follow the Boys*, with Marlene
Dietrich taking Rita's place.**

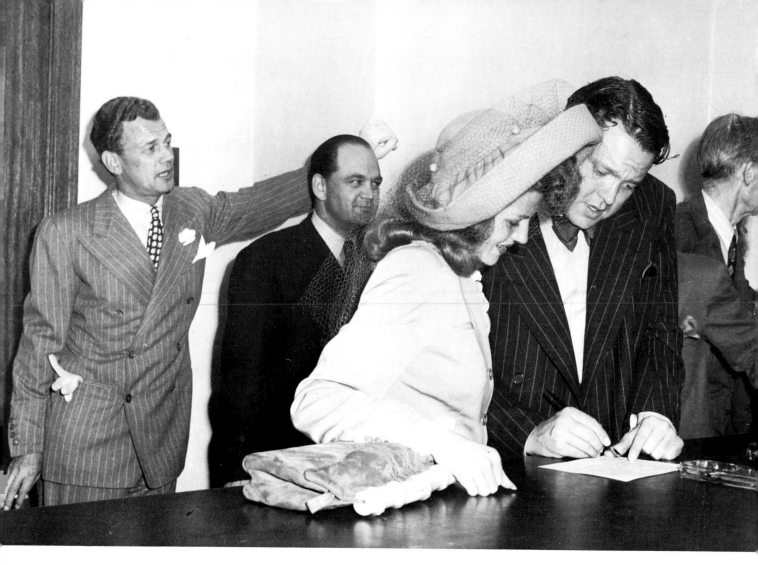

offering Welles any more romantic leads. Reading Antoine de Saint-Exupéry's sophisticated fairy story *The Little Prince* in proof, he fell in love with it and its film possibilities, and acquired the film rights before publication. The only trouble with the property was that it would need, however simply it was done, some quite complicated effects of animation. Walt Disney was the obvious person to undertake them, but when Welles arranged to meet Disney and discuss the project, they did not hit it off, and that was the end of that. (Welles subsequently resold the rights at a profit; they were to pass through several hands before the story finally arrived on screen in 1974 as a Lerner and Loewe musical of the same name, directed by Stanley Donen.)

This was all very frustrating. However, Welles did win one round of the Hollywood game when on 7 September 1943 he married Rita Hayworth, more or less over Harry Cohn's dead body. As they settled down to a, by current Hollywood standards, fairly quiet domestic life, with little partying or other frivolous distraction, Welles was at this time writing a regular political column (fairly naive

and flag-waving) for Dolivet's magazine *Free World*, something sufficiently leftish to get him into a bit of trouble later on, in the days of the McCarthy witch-hunts, though it was still difficult to imagine him, whatever his vague liberal sympathies, as in any way a Communist sympathizer. He also had a new radio show, *Orson Welles's Almanac*, in which he was able to indulge his recurrent fantasy of being a comedian – though, truth to tell, the special gifts of a Jack Benny or a Bob Hope were never part of his repertoire as a performer, least of all when he was writing his own material. And then there were shows to be done pushing war bonds, and all sorts of vaguely charitable activities, so that although he was doing little of long-term significance (or perhaps partly because of that) the usually robust and resilient Welles was pushed to the brink of mental and physical collapse, and ordered for the first time in his adult life to take a complete rest.

Meanwhile Rita was going from film to film, becoming a bigger box-office attraction with each. To do him justice, Welles does not seem to have felt threatened by his wife's success – probably his ego was too big to permit it. In

early 1944 she found she was pregnant, and when she had finished work on *Tonight and Every Night*, a musical salute to wartime London, she settled down to await the baby. His first wife, Virginia, chose this time to sue Welles on behalf of his first child, Christopher, to make sure that her interests were protected however many more children Welles might have, and though Welles was much upset by the case, matters were settled amicably enough, if expensively for him. Around this time also he accepted an offer from impresario Billy Rose to direct a comedy by Donald Ogden Stewart, *Emily Brady*, on stage in San Francisco and New York: it was not much of a challenge, but it would be lucrative. However, that fell through, through no fault of Welles's, owing to casting difficulties, and again he was left waiting for work. To fill some of the gap, he took on another job as a popular political columnist, this time five days a week, for the *New York Post*. And on 17 December 1944 his second child was born, also a daughter, and named Rebecca.

For the moment Welles's marriage seemed to be happy, but almost everything else was going wrong. He took a strictly acting job starring opposite Claudette Colbert in Irving Pichel's weepie *Tomorrow is Forever*, yet another variation on the *Enoch Arden* story in which Welles plays a handsome young husband (with a handsome false nose) who goes off to war and is believed to be dead, but comes back later, after being horribly wounded and transformed by plastic surgery (so that now he has his own nose) to find that his wife has remarried and just like everybody else fails to recognize him – which, with Orson Welles of all people (even given some shuffling of noses), is uniquely difficult to believe. Nor did Welles's bored and offhand performance make it any easier. Meanwhile he proved unable to sell radio sponsors on the idea of his delivering a regular political commentary on the air. But around this time CBS began to re-run his old Mercury Theatre on the Air programmes,

already regarded as classics, and showed an interest in getting him to do some new drama broadcasts along the same lines. For unexplained reasons *This Is My Best*, adapted, directed by and starring Welles lasted only seven weeks, and was then abruptly cancelled. But in those seven weeks he was able to give his most mature thoughts on *The Heart of Darkness*, to be dashing in *The Master of Ballantrae*, comical in *A Diamond as Big as the Ritz*, and to get back at Disney with his own version of *Snow White*.

Maybe at this unsatisfactory juncture of his life, with all his show-business projects frustrated, Welles did manage to convince himself that his future might lie in politics, that he could give up the cinema and the theatre and find fulfilment elsewhere. He seriously considered standing for the Senate, but decided that anyone who did so, secretly harboured an ambition to enter 'the big building' and he 'didn't think anyone could be elected President who had been divorced and who had been an actor'.

At the urging of Dolivet he continued to make political speeches and to write his political columns, though the *New York Post* soon tactfully suggested that the public was not really very interested in his political ideas and would rather read him discussing show-business topics, if not actually dishing the dirt on Hollywood. For a while he did a radio talk-show centred on the soon-to-be founded United Nations and its originators, which worked well enough – no one ever doubted Welles's know-how as a radio journalist – and when he had a topic, usually not too narrowly political, which really moved him, like the death of Roosevelt, he could be eloquent indeed. But he always seemed like an actor playing a politician, and though he sometimes played the role very well, he could always switch to something else at a moment's notice. When he did finally hit upon a formula which worked for a radio comment programme (which was in September 1945), it was very soon clear that it worked not because of Welles's political message or any faith listeners might have in him as a guru, but because, like so many radio and television personalities who succeeded him, he was a provocative, unpredictable person, an Ancient Mariner whose golden voice (even without the glittering eye) could hold an audience enthralled even if he chose to recite extracts from the New York telephone directory. Since he was no fool, he quickly took note that it was not what he said, but the way that he said it – and let his public personality develop from there.

And there was, finally, another chance to direct in Hollywood coming up. The conditions were far from what he would wish, but at least it was a chance to prove that he didn't have to be a genius all the time – he could make a routine movie efficiently if he wanted to, just like ordinary Hollywood folks. Sam Spiegel, later best known as producer of *The Bridge on the River Kwai*, had *The Stranger*, a script by John Huston and Anthony Veiller, based on a story by Victor Trivas, about an ex-Nazi hiding out as an innocent-seeming schoolteacher in a small American town, which he was going to produce for a minor studio, International Pictures. He thought Welles would be perfect as the Nazi, and offered him the role. Welles liked the idea, and offered to direct as well. After some hesitation, Spiegel agreed, but on one condition: Welles could modify the script as much as he liked before shooting, but then he was to guarantee that not a thing would be changed once shooting had begun. Moreover Welles, with his unfortunate (and at this point largely undeserved) reputation for not finishing pictures, had to guarantee to pay International out of his own pocket should he default, and would get paid the bulk of his salary only once the film was finished. All this seemed pretty demeaning, but Welles was so eager to get back somehow to directing and make himself bankable again that he accepted all the conditions imposed upon him.

He stuck by them too. Spiegel noted wrily

Tomorrow is Forever. **Welles as a young soldier with Claudette Colbert and nose number one (left); as an invalid after plastic surgery, with Claudette Colbert, Richard Long, and nose number two (below).**

78

at the one day he had to leave town during the shooting, Welles immediately, and perhaps most involuntarily, changed everything shot that day, just a little but enough to show a spark of rebellion. All the same, the picture, which also starred Edward G. Robinson and Loretta Young, came in exactly on schedule and under budget. It was a straightforward film made quite inexpensively, and made its modest profit without setting any box-office records. It is certainly not as interesting as one would hope a Welles film to be, but it is crisp and stylish of its kind (Welles the director allows his own performance as an actor to go noticeably over the top), an effective minor *film noir* which is certainly not as bad as Welles (*The Stranger* is the worst of my films. There is nothing of me in that picture') and his more enthusiastic supporters have claimed. Of course, Welles also had a scapegoat: the editor Ernest Nims, whose attentions he regarded as entirely malevolent, here and in the later *Touch of Evil*. Nims, it seems, not only cut *The Stranger* to the bare bones of plot but gratuitously removed the one sequence Welles liked (and no one else has seen), a South American prologue dealing with the Nazi's escape before his arrival in the States, which Welles belatedly decided was wonderful.

But he seems to have got on well enough directing his stars, especially Loretta Young, who, when Robinson objected to being photographed on his 'bad side', readily volunteered, 'OK, shoot me on my bad side and keep him happy.' Welles later observed, 'the director has to carry on a continual courtship with the people he sticks in front of the lens,' (even Edward G. Robinson!), but he clearly accepted this as a part of cinematic life.

At least *The Stranger*, whatever Welles eventually thought of it, did give him back a bit of Hollywood credibility as a director. Not perhaps the sort he wanted, the sort which would let him loose with the whole toy-box again; but people would not laugh in his face any more at the very idea he might be allowed

to direct, or groan when he brought out the footage of *It's All True* one more time. (This, incidentally, he for the moment had in his possession, having signed away all his rights in *Citizen Kane* and the unmade third picture for RKO in order to get it, as well as promising an extra $200,000, which he was eventually forced to default on. Typically, once he had won that particular battle he paid little further

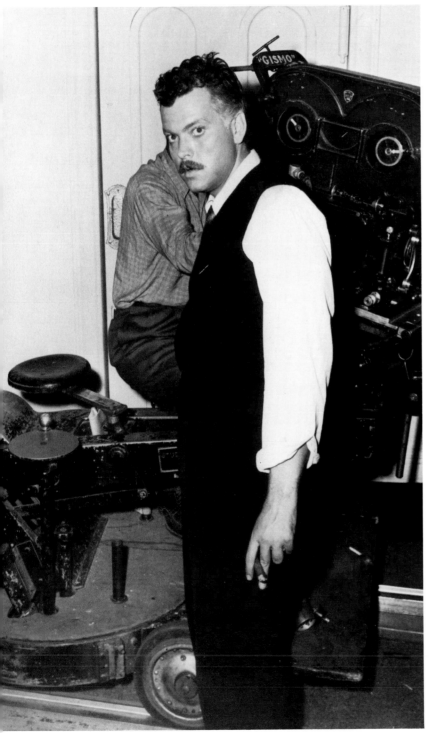

Welles agreed to play the heavy in *The Stranger* and direct it without deviation from the agreed script. He got on well with co-star Loretta Young, less well with Edward G Robinson (who for once plays the good guy).

attention to its ostensible cause.) His marriage was in and out of trouble – Rita was inclined to irrational jealousy, even before Welles started to give her ample reason – but he was too occupied with, at last, a new Broadway show to worry much about that, and when Rita, back in Hollywood in the middle of shooting *Gilda*, announced unilaterally that they were separating, it came as a real shock to him.

However, one thing at a time (or at least no more than two, since he was still working on the last details of *The Stranger*). One of his long-standing, nebulous schemes was to adapt *Around the World in Eighty Days* somehow to stage or screen. It was one of those popular classics he had first tackled in The Mercury Theatre on the Air (like so many of his later projects), and he somehow thought of it as his own property, like *War and Peace*, which Korda had been claiming for some years Welles would direct after the war with himself as Pierre, Vivien Leigh as Natasha and Laurence Olivier as Andrei, though it always seemed unlikely that either of these fantasist-showmen would ever bring the idea to birth. John Houseman says, 'Orson has established proprietory rights on film versions of most of the world's classics,' and no doubt *Around the World in Eighty Days* would have remained in that limbo if another showman-dreamer, with a more practical turn of mind, had not intervened.

This was Mike Todd, who after having his successes with *The Hot Mikado* and Maurice Evans's *Hamlet* was now going through his cultural phase. Somehow, late in 1945, Welles and Todd, by a species of *folie à deux*, had decided that a version of the Jules Verne story adapted and directed by Welles, with songs by Cole Porter, could be at once a cultural triumph and a Broadway smash. When Rita delivered her bombshell Welles was in the East, conferring with Cole Porter, and during the next four months, while they wrangled vaguely over the divorce settlement, he was living and

working mostly in New York. This kept him near the centre of things for *Around the World*, but made negotiations over his other theatrical plans inordinately difficult. They were to direct, with Todd producing, the first production of Brecht's *Galileo*, with Charles Laughton, who had worked with Brecht on the elaboration of the English text, starring. A quartet such as Brecht, Welles, Laughton and Todd would be difficult enough to control at the best of times, even more so when two were on the West Coast and two on the East, largely preoccupied with something else. To complicate matters further, Welles did not like Brecht or the composer, Hanns Eisler, and their ideas on theatre (apart from a shared dislike of theatrical realism) could hardly have been more different. Brecht and Laughton, for their part, felt that the Welles / Todd approach was much too extravagant and 'Broadway', and in any case had endless trouble tying either of their potential collaborators down to specifics. Then, on

the eve of *Around the World*'s Boston try-out, Mike Todd, exasperated by the ever-escalating expenses of Welles's production, withdrew, and so Welles and Todd were not speaking any more, though each individually remained interested, or so he said, in *Galileo*. But Brecht and Laughton despaired of ever getting satisfactorily together with their warring ex-partners, and instead, to Welles's fury, looked to Joseph Losey to direct and John Houseman and Norman Lloyd (formerly of the Mercury Theatre) to produce.

Welles, anyway, had quite enough on his plate. Unwisely deciding against postponing production on *Around the World*, now without any backers, he set about raising the necessary money himself, from his own dwindling resources, from Alexander Korda, from Harry Cohn (in return for a promise to make him a picture later in the year), and wherever else he could. The Boston opening was a total disaster, the stops in New Haven and Philadelphia hardly better, and Welles, who had not originally intended to appear in the show at all, found himself standing in sometimes as Phileas Fogg, sometimes as Passepartou (though fortunately never at the same performance). By New York he had decided officially to throw his weight as a performer into the balance, and taken on the role of Fogg's rival Dick Fix. For such a wildly complicated show, the Broadway opening went remarkably smoothly, but the critics were not impressed: 'It is mammoth, it is gigantic, it is lavish. It is also dull,' said the *New York Post*. Welles's longtime, Hearst-controlled enemy, the *Journal American*, tagged it as 'a show shown by a show-off, full of sets and costumes, signifying nothing in particular.' It limped on for nearly three months, owing entirely to Welles's determination and subsidies, and when it closed he was flat broke – worse, for he lost the *It's All True* footage to RKO into the bargain, being unable to pay the money he owed them.

Most of his other incidental careers were coming to an end too – his *New York Post* column, his political talk spot on ABC radio (though then he went down flags flying with a series of pieces about a racist police beating in the South which made big news, if few friends for him), and any of his remaining political ambitions. But there was still that film he had undertaken (under duress) to make for Harry Cohn. He had a property approved by Cohn – a tough thriller by Sherwood King, sub-Chandler stuff, called *If I Die Before I Wake* – and he intended to make a quick, unpretentious film out of it, shot largely on location in New York, starring a new French discovery of his own as the central femme fatale. This way he should be able to make a bit of money out of the (again very disadvantageous) contract he had been forced into, which gave him bare salary and the bulk of his money when, if ever, Columbia got back its initial investment. But Cohn had other ideas. New York was out, for one. And for another, he insisted on Welles's casting Rita Hayworth, still his wife despite

their separation, and Columbia's most valuable star.

It was generally assumed, then and subsequently, that Welles devised *The Lady from Shanghai* specifically as a vehicle (and probably gift of love) for Rita, while there were those who unkindly said that he saw his wife's enormous popularity as the only way he could get back into Hollywood after yet another disastrous flop. In fact, demonstrably, neither of these thoughts was in his mind, and he retained grave doubts about using Rita till the last. However, she welcomed the idea as offering a possibility of reconciliation – the more feasible since they had both been hanging back rather from proceeding with their divorce. And Welles was not after all averse to the extra box-office potential her presence in the film brought, or the publicity their reconciliation promoted (encouraged by shots of Welles trimming the luxuriant Hayworth tresses in preparation for her new image as a platinum blonde), or indeed, as it turned out, the reconciliation itself, for he still loved Rita even if he found it impossible to be faithful to her.

What one does wonder, looking at the finished film, is what on earth could have been going on in Welles's mind. It seems difficult to discount altogether the working of Welles's much-discussed, much-denied self-destructive urges. Can he ever really have meant to make a straightforward, unpretentious thriller, along the lines, presumably, of *The Stranger*, when his memos to Harry Cohn constantly stress the necessity to keep the film from being 'just another whodunit' by emphasizing the bizarre, oblique and off-centre? When questioned years later about the complexities of the film, he commented: 'I'm bored with stories that don't seem to be balanced dangerously . . . you walk down a highway with a story, instead of a tightrope. I'm bored with it.'

Attempts to justify or explain the film's peculiarities by discovering in it the influence of Brecht's dramatic theories hardly improve matters, since who in his right mind would

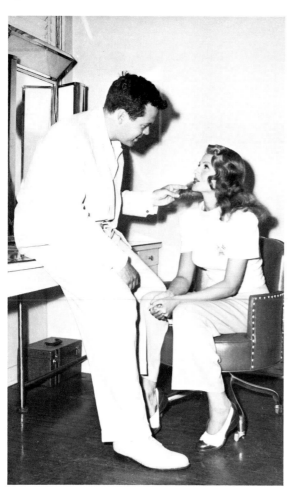

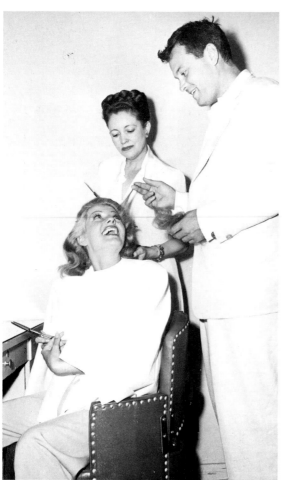

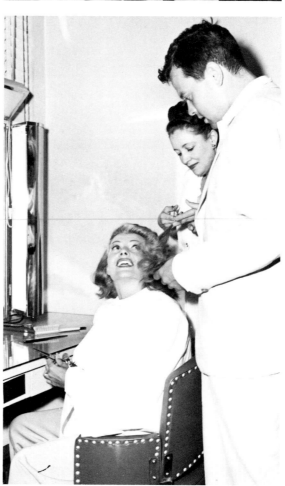

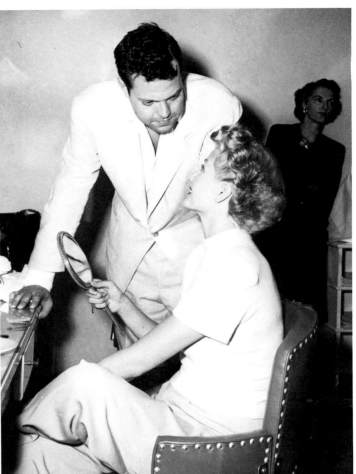

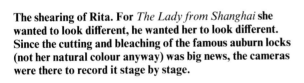

The shearing of Rita. For *The Lady from Shanghai* she wanted to look different, he wanted her to look different. Since the cutting and bleaching of the famous auburn locks (not her natural colour anyway) was big news, the cameras were there to record it stage by stage.

suppose (particularly in 1946) that a Brechtian effect would be accessible to the general public? (And if so, it only proves that the Devil can quote scripture for his own purposes, given Welles's total divergence from anything Brecht would have recognized or approved of.) Indeed the film makes most sense if we read it as in some way Welles's revenge on Hollywood for having to make *The Stranger*: forced to be direct and linear, was he? Well, we'll see just how obscure and disjointed he can be if he tries. But if so, whom was the revenge on? Welles was the only one to suffer, finding himself as a result a refugee from directing in major studios for another twelve years.

For the unfortunate truth about *The Lady from Shanghai* is that not only Harry Cohn failed to understand it when he got to see it; no one has certainly understood it, then or since. Of course Welles had his usual excuses: *they* ruined it. But even he did not suggest that the studio, in revising it, made it any more obscure, and he seemed to feel that *they* had done less damage to it than they did to several of his other films. It was almost as though he was proud (and this might be his Achilles heel) of its failure, as though he felt it would be an admission of defeat and dereliction of his intellectual duty to make a popular success, accessible to all. Through the years he said a lot about the vitality of the popular arts, the need to get through to a genuine mass audience. But when it came to doing so himself, a sort of intellectual snobbery seemed to hold him back: if an intellectual genius was caught out being actually understood and enjoyed, then so much less the intellectual genius he.

The result in *The Lady from Shanghai* – particularly unfortunate for something which is after all a Rita Hayworth movie as well as an Orson Welles film – is a disturbing sense of alienation in all the wrong senses rather than in the respectable Brechtian sense of the term. There are dazzling individual effects, but there is no appreciable centre to tie them all together, and before long one ceases to care who did

what to whom and what is going to happen anyway. The new, blonde, coldly mysterious Rita fails to displace the old red-haired version from the public consciousness – especially since she turns out improbably to be the villain in the final scenes. And Welles himself, as the tough innocent in the middle of all this obscure plotting, seems more lost for answers than anyone else – perhaps the writer-director did not bother to brief him. Cohn took one look at the film (which was by then half a million over budget) and ordered a tough re-editing job, to be carried out by an editor, Viola Lawrence, whom Welles insisted on regarding as a personal enemy, maliciously out to ruin him.

Though their marriage had held together reasonably well during shooting, when they were both totally preoccupied with the film,

Welles supervised every stage of production on *The Lady from Shanghai*, even to painting the grotesque masks himself. He probably sometimes felt very much like his image in the distorting mirror at the funfair. Opposite: pulling out all the stops on a publicity tour.

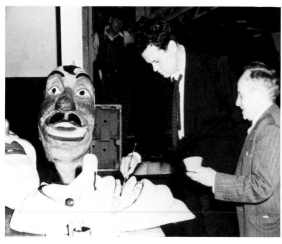

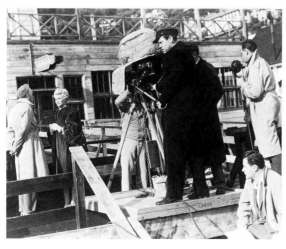

Rita now started making scenes again, Welles started philandering again, and the relationship was clearly not to be resurrected again.

Even at this point Welles does not seem to have written off completely his chances with Cohn, whom, in spite of everything, he seems rather to have liked, overcome by his established taste for monsters. He even enthusiastically outlined to Cohn a notion for filming *Carmen*, the original gutsy novel rather than the opera, as a vehicle for Rita. Cohn listened and took note, but when he came to follow up the idea he very naturally gave the film to someone else. Welles had clearly tried the patience of Hollywood too far, almost deliberately ruining his second chance as he had, much more innocently, ruined his first. Retreat seemed the only possibility: back to the theatre, perhaps, if anyone would have him after *Around the World in Eighty Days*. Or even further, ancestrally back to Europe, where after all they were supposed to appreciate and encourage the artist. As though in answer to his unspoken thought, a tempting offer came from his old friend and fellow fantasist Alexander Korda. Though no more was said of the plans for *War and Peace* (too complicated, apart from anything else, to shoot in Russia with the world now on the brink of the Cold War), Korda wanted him to make three pictures (unspecified) in England as soon as he had finished *The Lady from Shanghai*. It was in this context that Welles first thought of *Carmen*, as a vehicle for Paulette Goddard (already in England to make *An Ideal Husband* for Korda). He also thought of doing the *Master of Ballantrae* over again on film, and of reviving his *Cyrano* plans. And then Korda came up with the rights of Oscar Wilde's *Salome*, with possibly Vivien Leigh as Salome and Welles or Laurence Olivier as Herod. Well, with so many possibilities something good was bound to come of it. So why not leave far behind the Hollywood that signally failed to love and understand him, and head off into the sunrise, to begin a new and grander career in Europe?

*The world's
rejected
guest*

5

WHY NOT EUROPE INDEED? THE ONLY TROUBLE was that Korda was almost as difficult to keep to his plans as Welles himself. It was partly Welles's fault that delays in *The Lady from Shanghai* had forced the postponement of shooting on *Salome*, for which Welles already had a complete script, if no cast, from the impossible 1 January 1947 to a conceivably possible 1 April. But then Korda postponed again, at least until July, and Welles found himself with nothing specific to do. But there were possibilities, because although Broadway and Hollywood were not offering work, he had been receiving vague overtures from thoroughly non-commercial theatrical organizations to do something classical – most insistently to stage Shakespeare for the Utah Centennial Festival in Salt Lake City. Now that he would unexpectedly be free to do it, he agreed, toying with the idea of *King Lear*, which coincidentally he had been asked to film in England. Then he suddenly changed his mind. He would do *Macbeth* instead, get his ideas and his production in shape on stage, then take it all back to Hollywood camera-ready and film it there.

If the idea sounded unlikely, he came up with an even more unlikely backer. Herbert J. Yates, who owned and ran Republic Pictures, kept it going little if at all above poverty row standards, except that he might splash out a slightly larger budget when his adored wife, the Czech ex-skater Vera Hruba Ralston, was the star. But in the late forties he too, like Mike Todd, suddenly underwent a bout of culture, and began to finance (modestly, it is true) the productions of John Ford's independent company Argosy Pictures, like *Rio Grande* and his biggest hit *The Quiet Man*, Borzage's *Moonrise*, Milestone's *Red Pony* and a few other oddities. When Welles came to him with *Macbeth* he had scarcely embarked on this programme, but he was impressed by the possibility it offered for getting a new, cultured audience and, even more, by the extraordinary economy with which Welles said he could make

it. Three weeks' black-and-white shooting, a budget less than $900,000, and a cast with no names in it except Welles – he could hardly go far wrong. So he agreed, and Hollywood was gratified by the weird prospect of its most ambitious and unmanageable director getting together with its cheapest studio to make the first American attempt at filmed Shakespeare since Reinhardt's gorgeous but financially disastrous *Midsummer Night's Dream* in 1935.

What Welles had in mind, or so he claimed, was an experiment in making a cheap, quickly made 'repertory' film which would stand in relation to a Hollywood superproduction as a 'straw hat' production in the theatre did to a Broadway spectacular. A certain fault of logic could be pointed out even then – a film, however quickly and cheaply made, sticks around to be reassessed long after a small stage production is gone and forgotten – but it was an interesting notion, bound to keep Welles in the news while *The Lady from Shanghai* languished on Columbia's shelves, not to be shown in the US till almost eighteen months after completion. Welles rehearsed the principals of his cast in Los Angeles, then moved up to Utah and recruited the minor characters locally, only to replace them with Hollywood professionals when he moved back to Republic in June to shoot the film. In addition to himself he had Dan O'Herlihy, later Buñuel's Robinson Crusoe, as Macduff, Roddy McDowall as Malcolm, his elder daughter Christopher as one of Macduff's children, his first wife's second husband Charles Lederer as a witch, and, failing Tallulah Bankhead, a seasoned radio actress called Jeanette Nolan as Lady Macbeth.

To everyone's amazement, shooting went exactly according to plan, completed in twenty-one days and under budget. Welles had proved that he could work under tight controls even when it was he himself who was doing the controlling. Herbert J. Yates was ecstatic, and even his enemies were impressed. Now all he needed was to edit and do the post-production work,

and all would be plain sailing. There couldn't be any problem with that – or could there? For what followed one can only call into play again Welles's alleged self-destructive streak. He felt he deserved a holiday. He had to go to Europe to confer with Korda on the forthcoming film of *Cyrano*, which had now been moved up to first place in the schedule. He needed money meanwhile, and let himself be talked into appearing in a piece of extravagant nonsense variously called *Black Magic* or *Cagliostro*, which his faintly disreputable friend Gregory Ratoff was to direct in Italy that autumn. But he could have done all these things and still completed *Macbeth* satisfactorily in good time. However, when he got back to Hollywood he dragged his heels over the editing and spent more time practising swordplay for his forthcoming role as the shady eighteenth-century magician. The truth was, he had got bored with *Macbeth* and just walked away, pretending because it suited his purposes that he believed all the essential work was in the shooting, and anyone could edit the film – he who had com-

plained bitterly about the slightest modification in his editing on all his other films.

If that is not self-destructiveness, what is? He rapidly lost all the good points he had made on his speedy and efficient shooting. Republic understandably became more and more enraged when he insisted all the unedited material must be shipped with his editor to Italy, and then commandeered the editor for *Cagliostro*, a large part of which he was unofficially directing himself, only to send *Macbeth* back late and still uncompleted. If he wanted to convince anybody he was responsible and disciplined and safe to entrust with a major Hollywood production again, he was certainly not going the right way about it. Nor were his 'serious' prospects in Europe any more promising. He kept on hopefully preparing *Cyrano* until Korda told him he intended to sell the rights of the property to America for ready money; he, like Orson, was always in severe financial straits. *Salome*, *The Master of Ballantrae* and the rest seemed to have gone up in smoke. But in Italy the living was relatively easy for visiting

Macbeth, made on a shoestring for the shoestring studio, Republic. As head of Republic, Herbert J Yates shakes Welles's hand before the assembled cast (opposite); he seems awed and Welles mischievous. When the film finally came out, critics opined that apart from Welles's own performance as Macbeth, the production had not got far enough away from its impoverished origins. Welles off set (right) with a young Natalie Wood.

Welles visits Alexander Korda on the set of *Anna Karenina* to discuss possible projects. Opposite: Welles at his hammiest having a ball with the role of the magician Cagliostro in *Black Magic*.

American celebrities, so why should Welles ever go back home?

Inevitably, he had a new film project – he always had another new film project. This time it arose from an almost casual suggestion made to him in Venice by an Italian film producer: why did he not do his own version of *Othello* on location there? Always susceptible to the flattery of anyone else wanting him to do anything, Welles immediately fell in with the idea, even if the producer almost as immediately fell out with it. Though he should have learnt his lesson from *It's All True*, he decided he could easily finance the film himself from what he could earn acting in other people's films – conceivably he somehow felt he had to make it work this time just to prove that he had not been a total idiot the time before. In a fairly light-hearted spirit he began drumming up acting work to get the directorial work started, and with Darryl Zanuck's help almost immediately landed the role of Cesare Borgia in the Rome-made *Prince of Foxes*, a swashbuckler starring Tyrone Power.

Obviously at this point he did not fully realize what he was getting himself into: some three years of intermittent work, stopping and starting and recasting and reshooting and patching up the editing somehow to hide the great unavoidable gaps in the continuity, and all the time struggling desperately to make ends meet, paying actors and technicians when he didn't really need them and couldn't use them, just to keep them with the film and reasonably happy. The wonder is that he got *Othello* finished at all, though probably it was all the opposition of fate and circumstance that drove him from sheer cussedness to do it: there never was anything like the challenge of the impossible to strengthen his resolve, while conversely if something came too easily he was all too likely to lose interest.

As with his *Macbeth*, for instance. Poor unloved one, it was finally completed in time

**Another colourful acting role in someone else's film:
Welles plays Cesare Borgia opposite Tyrone Power in
Henry King's swashbuckler** *Prince of Foxes.*

to show in the Venice Festival of August 1948.
It was to be in competition, but some instinct
persuaded Welles to pull it out and make it a
non-competitive entry just before the festival
began. Probably he felt it would not show well
in direct comparison with Olivier's glossy,
meditated, big-budget *Hamlet*, which was also
in the festival. But he can never have imagined
the incomprehension and naked hostility with
which it was received. People did not like anything about it, from the shoddy sets, which
made it all appear to take place in a cave left
over from *One Million BC* (made in 1940), and
the improvised costumes, to the poverty-
stricken crowd scenes and the very variable and
lackadaisical acting, reasonable repertory standard at best. The more sophisticated spectators
recognized that it was meant to be stylized, but
felt it was not stylized enough, trying sadly to
dissimulate its poverty of means instead of
making a virtue of simplicity. The fiercest criticism was reserved for the soundtrack, all
spoken in a variety of weird American approx-
imations to a Scottish accent which were to
foreigners incomprehensible and to the British
laughable. Welles was shattered, and (of
course) put it all down to personal enmity and
spite. Republic immediately snatched the film
from distribution and set about the expensive
and ineffectual process of redubbing most of
the track in something nearer to standard
English. From being a cheap write-off it had
escalated into a quite expensive write-off, and
Welles's name was anathema. Moreover, this
time he really had no one to blame but himself.

However, he soldiered on with *Othello*,
which now became his necessary proof that he
could bring Shakespeare successfully to the
screen. With his money from *Prince of Foxes*
he shot a number of scenes in Venice, with himself as Othello and Everett Sloane, from *Kane*
and *Ambersons*, as Iago. It was good casting,
by all accounts (Welles said privately that
Sloane was so jealous of his looks anyway . . .),
but eventually Sloane could not afford to hang
around any longer, and left the cast. So now

Welles had to scrap almost all the shot footage,
find a new Iago, and also find a new
Desdemona, since he had second thoughts
about his original choice, the Italian actress
and soon-to-be-ex-friend Lea Padovani. He
also had to find more money, and so took the
next acting job that offered, after holding out
for a generous fee for what was after all a very
short though important role. The film, produced by his old almost-associate Alexander
Korda, was *The Third Man*, directed by Carol
Reed in Vienna: it was going to provide Welles,
in less than ten minutes' screen time, with the
role he would be most instantly associated with
for the rest of his life. Indeed, when his death
was announced it was *The Third Man* which
British television immediately put on as his
memorial.

The villainous Harry Lime, amoral drug-dealer in war-torn Vienna, became, curiously, one of Welles's most famous roles, even though he was actually on screen in *The Third Man* for less than ten minutes. On the preceding pages he is seen in several of those ten, as a shadow on a wall, in friendly conversation with Joseph Cotten, the innocent old friend who finally betrays him, and at bay in the sewers. Below and opposite: the final chase in the sewers, with Carol Reed directing.

There has been a lot of rumour and speculation about Welles's influence on *The Third Man* – a situation which he wilfully did little to clarify. In point of fact he was only around for about ten days of the shooting, the length of time it took to shoot his one big dialogue sequence, on the Big Wheel, the final chase in the sewers and his single other, wordless, one-shot appearance in the film. Graham Greene says that Welles suggested the famous line of dialogue: 'In Italy for thirty years under the Borgias they had warfare, terror, murder, bloodshed – they produced Michelangelo, Leonardo da Vinci, the Renaissance. In Switzerland they had brotherly love, five hundred years of democracy and peace, and what did that produce? The cuckoo clock.' And possibly his mere presence had some influence on the way the chase was shot. But it would be a bold man who could swear, after carefullly examining Reed's two previous films, *Odd Man Out* and *The Fallen Idol*, that there is anything in the film directorially that he could not possibly have invented, so Welles must have. Admittedly Welles liked later on to refer to *The Third Man* as 'my film' and insisted he wrote all the dialogue for his own part, but he was always prone to exaggeration. He categorically denied in a 1984 television interview that he had anything to do with the film's direction: 'There are a whole lot of things I'm supposed to have said, that come from my not hearing too well, or not being as good a linguist as I pretend to be.'

With the money he made from *The Third Man* he was soon back again working on *Othello*. He found a new Iago in his old friend (or in his view enemy) Micheal MacLiammoir, and a Desdemona in the young French actress Cécile Aubry, who had just had a big success in the controversial French film *Manon*, and after a couple of days' shooting went off to capitalize on it more practically in the American spectacular *The Black Rose*, whither Welles shortly followed her for exactly the same reason.

Welles in British studios. Above: visiting Ralph
Richardson and Michele Morgan on the set of *The Fallen
Idol*, the film directed immediately before *The Third Man*.
Below: chatting with Cary Grant and Ann Sheridan during
the making of Howard Hawks's *I was a Male War-Bride*.

Welles did not actually begin shooting the definitive version of *Othello* until June 1949, on location in Morocco, after rehearsals in Rome and Paris. He still had no Desdemona, but did not allow that to deter him. The extraordinary, erratic course of the shooting is vividly described by Micheal MacLiammoir in his diary of the film *Put Money in Thy Purse*, for which Welles wrote a very amicable introduction – something he would hardly have done if they were in fact at daggers drawn all the time. Early in August shooting moved back to Venice, with at least a Desdemona, a French-Canadian beauty called Suzanne Cloutier. Another break for more fund-raising, and then further shooting in Morocco from January to March 1950. By then most of the film was in the can, but there were always bits that could be improved or that it would be nice to add if they could be managed, not to mention the formidable post-production expenses to be paid out of Welles's own money and any he could beg or borrow.

Needless to say, this abiding worry did not prevent him from taking on other projects. The next world classic he meant to tackle was *The Odyssey*, which he proposed to start shooting right in the middle of *Othello*, though with what financing nobody knew. Then he had, whatever he said, been getting on so well with Micheal MacLiammoir and Hilton Edwards that he roped them in for a little theatrical venture he had in mind for Paris later in 1950: a weird combination of his own cut-down, revamped version of *Doctor Faustus* under the title *Time Runs*, and a one-act play of his own, a satire on Hollywood called *The Unthinking Lobster*, which later came out as a novel in French under the title *Une Grosse Légume*. The double bill at least made a pleasingly bizarre entertainment for Welles's many French admirers, even if they found quite a bit of difficulty in understanding it. The biggest personal success was scored by a dusky beauty called Eartha Kitt, who was singing in a Parisian cabaret when she was summoned by Welles to be his Helen of Troy. Though Welles was pleased with his discovery's success, he did not care to be upstaged in his own show, so much of the run was taken up by both *monstres sacrés* using every trick in the book to keep as much audience attention as possible for themselves. When Welles decided to take *Time Runs* on tour in Germany (rather than taking it to London), he replaced Hilton Edwards with Micheal MacLiammoir as his Mephistopheles, and dropped *The Unthinking Lobster* in favour of a weird miscellany containing great speeches from Shakespeare (delivered by Welles), three songs (delivered by Eartha Kitt), and a potted (very potted) version of *The Importance of Being Earnest*. No wonder the Germans were, though enthusiastic, bemused.

Funds having again run out, with most of the cutting on *Othello* still to do, Welles turned in 1951 to London, where he picked up money by doing a silly but popular radio series based on the character of Harry Lime, who had meanwhile been insensibly converted into a real nice guy, and kudos by presenting his *Othello* on the stage of the St James's Theatre under the management of Laurence Olivier (though the influential young British critic Kenneth Tynan neatly rubbished it by labelling it 'Citizen Coon'). At the same time, Welles assisted Hilton Edwards with a little filmed ghost story he was making, *Return to Glennascaul*, by narrating it and introducing himself in the midst of rehearsal for *Othello*, by way of a prologue. More British radio jobs followed, and finally in 1952 *Othello* was ready for showing at the Cannes Film Festival. It had a great success, and shared the Grand Prix with Castellani's *Due Soldi di Speranza*. This was satisfying, even if it did not guarantee the film a prompt showing – it did not open in the States for three years, or Britain for four. But at least Welles could feel satisfied that at last he had managed to make a film without outside interference, for the first time since *Citizen Kane*, and had imposed his own personal mark on screen Shakespeare, partly by taking it for

During the long-drawn-out process of filming *Othello*, with himself as Othello, Suzanne Cloutier as Desdemona and Micheal MacLiammoir as Iago. Welles worked on location in Venice and Morocco, gathering finance where and when he could.

granted that everyone knows the story, so you do not have to waste any more energy telling it in detail than you would in, say, a ballet version. The film is, at the very least, visually unforgettable, and provides a better correlative for Shakespeare's poetry than most ploddingly literal readings ever manage to achieve.

The great effort of *Othello* at last over, Welles was left for once without any immediate project, except a possible *Julius Caesar*, to be made in Egypt, which was promptly cancelled when John Houseman announced his Hollywood version, to be directed by Joseph L. Mankiewicz with Marlon Brando, 'the new Orson Welles', as Mark Antony. However, the old Orson Welles (all of thirty-eight) was not doing too badly. He appeared in more foolish pictures to make money fast, the first of them, *Trent's Last Case*, allegedly because its British director Herbert Wilcox had been the only one on the RKO lot in 1940 actually to like *Citizen Kane* in preview. (The story even went that because of this Welles had impulsively promised to do anything Wilcox might want of him for free – but of course by 1953 he could not afford to act in other people's films for anything but money.) He did *King Lear* for CBS television under the direction of Peter Brook. He wrote a script for a Roland Petit ballet, *The Lady in the Ice*, and designed it. He wrote two novels which appeared first in French, *Une Grosse Légume* and a complicated thriller about a mysterious and criminal millionaire, *Mr Arkadin*. He endeared himself even further to the French by playing cameo roles in two of Sacha Guitry's all-star historical extravaganzas, *Si Versailles m'était Conté* and *Napoléon*. He even played quite his most unlikely role ever, appearing vastly kilted (Trucolor by Consolidated) as a Latin-American laird in a second Herbert Wilcox film, *Trouble in the Glen*.

But behind the scenes of all this he was plotting his next important moves: a major theatrical production and a major film. In 1954 the film, based on his novel *Mr Arkadin* and some-

times known as that, sometimes as *Confidential Report*, went into production. In summer 1955, when the film was just about to open in London, Welles put on his own play *Moby Dick – Rehearsed*, the last, as it would prove to be, of his real theatrical triumphs. This was also in London, where at this stage in his career he seemed to be a lot more at home than in New York – indeed, continuing arguments with the American tax authorities had made it difficult for him to go back to America, and his brief stint in New York recording the television *King Lear* had been managed only after a lot of delicate negotiation.

The circumstances of production on *Mr Arkadin* show how rootless and cosmopolitan Welles had become in the last six years. He had become a gypsy, wandering from place to place where the work was, and without any permanent place of residence. Since his decisive break with Rita after *The Lady from Shanghai* (and despite a couple of belated attempts on her part to patch things up before their divorce became final and she married Ali Khan instead) he had not lacked for female companionship, but had entered into no long-term relationships – not until 1954, when he met an Italian countess and small-time actress called Paola Mori, whom he decided to star in his new film and who in due course was to become Mrs Orson Welles number three. The film's script was based on Welles's novel, which was really from the start a film treatment in disguise. It was inspired by various mysterious rich men Welles had met during his European wanderings, and assumed a form rather similar to that of *Citizen Kane*, except that in this instance the inquiry into the true history and nature of the gargantuan Arkadin (Welles had by this time put on an enormous amount of weight) is commissioned by himself, with, as it eventually emerges, the purpose of running to earth all the surviving people who know anything incriminating about him and somehow disposing of them so that his beloved daughter (Paola Mori) shall never learn the truth.

Welles as the mysterious financier in his own *Mr Arkadin*, alias *Confidential Report*. Below, he is seen with his discovery, Robert Arden, and, to far right, Paola Mori, who plays his daughter in the film and was soon to be wife number three. Opposite: two relaxed off-set moments with Paola Mori.

Again Welles determined that the film should be independently financed, so that he would not be subject to the constraints of conventional studio production (that is, supposing any studio would undertake to bank-roll him at this point), but he was tired of raising all the money himself, and called instead on his old friend and political mentor Louis Dolivet to join him as executive producer, with no creative responsibility but merely the task of raising money as and when needed. Production was centred on Madrid, where Dolivet managed to set up a co-production deal with a Spanish company, and over eight months in 1954 an extraordinary cast of internationally famous actors converged on the Madrid studios, each playing – for this was the joy of the thing – a short but impressive cameo role as his or her character emerged in the course of the investigator's investigations. On these terms Welles was able to lure such as Katina Paxinou, Michael Redgrave, Akim Tamiroff (rapidly to become a Welles regular), Patricia Medina, Susanne Flon, Gert Fröbe, Mischa

Auer, Peter van Eyck and Grégoire Aslan to take part, all at minimal cost. Apart from Arkadin himself, the only other major role running all through the film was that of the mysteriously hired investigator, played by Robert Arden, a London-based American whom Welles had encountered in his *Harry Lime* radio series. Arden was in fact summoned to Madrid almost as mysteriously as his character in the film: he was appearing in the London production of *Guys and Dolls* when he received a peremptory phone call from Welles, and within four days he had been bought out of the show (Carol Reed acting as Welles's intermediary), shipped off to Spain and pitchforked into the first scene of the picture.

Welles for once seemed to be having everything his own way – perhaps too much so for the peace of his restless mind, since he kept rewriting and restructuring the script from day to day, until no one was quite sure what they were doing, possibly not even him. (If he was not inevitably working on a brink, he had to create one.) He seems to have led the faithful

110

Dolivet quite a dance, running hither and thither and selling slices of the picture here, there and everywhere to raise the necessary cash – a process which finally ended the friendship and concluded the film in a welter of legal actions alleging undue delay and negligence on Welles's part, as well as unprofessional behaviour in hiring his latest girlfriend for a key role. (Though if that were unprofessional behaviour it is difficult to know who in Hollywood would remain immune to the charge.) Notwithstanding, as far as anyone knew at the time the film emerged in all its kaleidoscopic strangeness as very much what Welles wanted, and it was only much later that he began to deliver complaints and disclaimers: he told his official biographer Barbara Leaming in 1984, 'They took it away from me! And they completely destroyed the movie! More completely than any other picture of mine has been hurt by anybody, *Arkadin* was destroyed because they com-

pletely changed the entire form of it: the whole order of it, the whole point of it . . . *Ambersons* is *nothing* compared to *Arkadin*.' How much of that is true is very difficult to judge, but when one looks at the film's Chinese box of flashbacks within flashbacks, its very intricate and carefully calculated structure, the mind boggles at what Welles can originally have intended if *this* is much more linear. And, not knowing of Welles's reservations, many Welles experts have found the film totally characteristic of him at his best. On the other hand, many then and since – and this is possibly what irked him – have found it to be just a mess, all baroque effect and very little intellectual or emotional substance.

Though Welles was equally high-handed with *Moby Dick* on stage, it seems to have been a far happier experience for almost all concerned, and Welles eventually opined that it was 'the best thing I ever did in *any* form – and

Welles in his London stage production *Moby Dick – Rehearsed*, with the 'cabin-boy', soon to be famous in her own right, Joan Plowright.

I seriously think that if I ever did anything really good, that was it.' At other times he said the same things, so perhaps the opinion should be taken with a pinch of salt; in any case it cannot now be checked. (Unless more exists than we have been led to suppose of the television film he was making of it and stopped after one day's shooting, or three days' shooting, or, if you believe the director of photography on it, considerably more.) While Welles was editing *Arkadin* in Paris he was asked by Michael Powell to appear in his updated version of *Die Fledermaus*, called *Oh Rosalinda!*, and agreed, but then could not be tied down: weeks later he surfaced again and was totally amazed that in his absence the role had had to be re-cast – how was it possible they had not waited and changed their schedule to suit him? But around the same time in Paris he made a very useful contact when he met the young British writer Wolf Mankowitz, through Carol Reed, who had filmed Mankowitz's book *A Kid for Two Farthings*. Mankowitz had recently gone into theatrical management in London with Oscar Lewenstein, and was enthused by Welles's talk of doing *King Lear* and his own dramatization of *Moby Dick* on the Paris stage. Why not do them in London? he asked. Welles was quite happy with the notion, and became even happier when Mankowitz managed to set up for him a series of six BBC Television programmes to be shot in Paris and called *The Orson Welles Sketchbook*, plus some well-paying writing assignments for British newspapers and magazines. Clearly this was someone with whom he could work.

Initially Mankowitz tried to set up the stage production with a more seasoned management than his own, but both Henry Sherek and the all-powerful H. M. Tennent turned them down – or *it* down, since the planned repertory season had narrowed itself to just *Moby Dick*. At this point, Mankowitz decided to present the show himself, getting finance for it from the New York management of Martin Gabel (who had last worked with Welles on *Danton's Death*)

Welles with John Huston (right) and playing the brief but showy role of Father Mapple in Huston's almost contemporary film version of *Moby Dick*.

and Henry Margolis, primarily on the assumption that after London and a provincial British tour Welles would take *Moby Dick* to New York. This suited everybody, since in London the play cost incredibly little to put on: Welles himself worked for a pittance, there was a lot of talent but no big names in the cast (though Gordon Jackson, Patrick McGoohan and a girl called Joan Plowright, who played a cabin boy, were to become big names soon enough), and the set and props were minimal, most of the effect being created by working on the audience's imagination. Even when Welles disconcerted his backers by announcing that four weeks was the maximum he was prepared to run it (the plan was for six or eight weeks), with no provincial tour and no New York season, they were not too worried, as the show got excellent notices and good if not sell-out audiences, so nobody for once stood to lose anything on Welles.

The idea of the production was brilliantly simple, like something Welles might have done in early Mercury days. Nothing like a full-dress spectacle would be attempted. Instead, we have the framework of a play within a play. A modest Victorian theatrical company are playing *King Lear* in the evenings and rehearsing their next production, *Moby Dick*, during the day, so what we are seeing is literally what the published text of the play was called, *Moby Dick – Rehearsed*. The setting is an empty stage, the props just such as might be lying round a Victorian theatre or be called for in *King Lear*. All the machinery is in the actors' imagination, and in ours. A large net of ropes hung from the flies is all we see to conjure up a full-rigged whaler, and the storm at sea is created entirely by the choreographed movements of the sailor-actors. Much of the rest, the creation of atmosphere and such, is managed by elaborate lighting – which in this production Welles entrusted to Hilton Edwards, a proven virtuoso. Welles himself was able, by the non-realistic form of the text, to play the company's actor-manager playing Captain Ahab, Father Mapple, and at odd moments King Lear as well. Though he sometimes doubted whether he was really right for Ahab – would not Patrick McGoohan, the Starbuck, be better – everyone else seemed fully satisfied and the notices were uniformly excellent: the critic Kenneth Tynan described it as 'a sustained assault on the senses, which dwarfs anything London has ever seen since, perhaps, the Great Fire . . . with it, the theatre becomes once more a house of magic.'

Welles was so pleased with Wolf Mankowitz as a partner that several more plans immediately took conversational form: Welles would direct Mankowitz's play *The Dark Dustman*; he and Mankowitz would collaborate on the writing and direction of a film based on Mankowitz's novel *The Mendelman Fire*, which would star Welles and Akim Tamiroff. The repertory season, before Welles dismissed it, was to include as well as *The Dark Dustman*, a Welles adaptation of Hemingway's *The Sun Also Rises*, starring Marlene Dietrich, and either *Volpone* or *Timon of Athens*. But again Welles soon lost interest and when the short run of *Moby Dick* was over he headed off to the continent to shoot material for a new television series, *Around the World with Orson Welles*, which had come up after the success of *The Orson Welles Sketchbook*. In any case it offered a useful escape, given Welles's doubts about the possibility of preparing *Moby Dick* adequately for New York in the three weeks offered. The unhappy interlude of *Around the World* apart, it was nearly fifteen years since Welles had worked in the New York theatre, and it had changed drastically. He knew, or believed, that American Equity members these days worked strictly by the rule book, and he would not be allowed to work as he had previously worked best, rehearsing all round the clock when the mood took him and making almost superhuman demands of his company. Also, even since 1946 the American theatre had changed radically with the ascendancy of the Actors Studio and the Method, all of which went right against Welles's own ideas on the actor as puppet and the primacy of the director: he was impatient enough with psychological niceties anyway, and was not likely to look with favour on having to divide his authority with an individual actor's coach, let alone his psychiatrist.

So Welles did not go to New York with *Moby Dick* in 1955. But in 1956 he was back anyway with his ultimate *King Lear* (if anything in his life was ultimate except his leaving of it – at which time he was seriously working on yet another attempt to film *Lear*, having now, he decided, arrived at the right age for it). New York and New York actors realized all his worst fears. He had planned to take over five thoroughly rehearsed British actors as the nucleus of his intended repertory company, but then discovered that American Equity would not permit this, and he had to cast again from scratch, at short notice, from those same by-the-book New York actors whose pettifogging ways and clock-watching he paranoically fantasized about and abhorred. To complicate matters Paola Mori, whom he had married in London the previous year, just before *Moby Dick* opened, was pregnant, and soon after their arrival in New York gave birth to a child, a third daughter for Welles, promptly christened Beatrice after Welles's mother. And then, by one of those Freudian slips so frequent in Welles's career, he broke one ankle just before first night and the other immediately after it.

The notices were middling to poor, despite the evident delight of the packed first-night audience at seeing him back at all. Never one to lose out on a chance of publicity, however

Welles and friends in the nightclub magic act he did in a
Las Vegas casino on his leisurely way back to Hollywood,
1957.

uncomfortably arrived at, on the second night Welles appeared on stage in a wheelchair, explained what had happened to his ankles, apologized for the impossibility of doing the play that night, and invited those of the audience who did not want their money back (which was to say nearly all of them) to stay for an informal Evening with Orson Welles. By the end of the week he was playing Lear, fully costumed and made-up, from his wheelchair and getting nightly ovations. Which was all very well, but did not lead to any extension of the production's limited run, and certainly did not produce any new backers for the hoped-for repertory company. Welles was back in America, but in most respects as much an outsider as ever.

However, he did have a bit of publicity in hand, and so before he went back to Europe he thought he might as well cash in on it. Typically, instead of doing anything which would give him 'dignity' and respect, he chose to go

Welles looks grim in the film with which he came back to Hollywood, as an actor only, Jack Arnold's *Pay the Devil*, otherwise called *Man in the Shadow*. His co-star was Jeff Chandler.

to Las Vegas and do cabaret for a month at the Riviera Hotel, mixing his old magic tricks with great speeches from *The Merchant of Venice* and *Julius Caesar* to entertain (very successfully, be it said) an audience of tired businessmen, blue-rinsed ladies and honeymoon couples. This had replenished his coffers a little when he went on to Hollywood, for the first time since the *Macbeth* débâcle, to star opposite Betty Grable in a television version of the old Hecht–MacArthur comedy *Twentieth Century*, in which he played the monomaniac actor-manager Oscar Jaffe, a role previously played with enormous success by his late, great friend John Barrymore (just another piece of type-casting, some might say).

Soon afterwards he was back directing again, though only in the most modest possible way, for the new medium, dreaded by most people in movies but which Welles found strangely appealing and manageable. Back in Paris he had already started work on an odd notion of making a half-hour television adaptation of an episode from *Don Quixote*, with Akim Tamiroff as Sancho Panza. He would eventually return to it. But now he received an offer from Desilu to make a pilot for a new series of adaptations which would be rather like a television equivalent of The Mercury Theatre on the Air: Welles would select, adapt, direct, narrate and on occasion appear in these half-hour films. The pilot, which he based on John Collier's short story 'Youth from Vienna', retitling it *The Fountain of Youth*, is curiously similar in tone to many of Alfred Hitchcock's *Half-Hours* – or not so curiously when we remember that the cynical Collier was one of Hitchcock's favourite authors also. In this story the inventor of an elixir of youth gives the fiancée who has jilted him enough of the potion as a wedding present to ensure either her or her tennis-player husband eternal youth, but not both of them, then sits back to watch them suffer. But Welles took a month to shoot his half-hour film (something not allowed even a genius in American television), as opposed

to the three days normal for Hitchcock, and incorporated so many spectacular effects of dialogue overlapping, cut-less transitions and such to tell his story of romantic revenge that on completion, the film was judged terminally uncommercial and shelved for two years before turning up in an off-season miscellany of unsold pilots and unexpectedly carrying off the 1958 Peabody Award for Excellence. Too late to do Welles any good, of course . . .

But he went on working. He added to the long list of directorial non-starters a script by Charles Lederer (to whom, incidentally, the first Mrs Orson Welles was no longer married) called *Tip on a Dead Jockey*, which MGM toyed with for a moment. And he agreed to pay his bills by working as an actor in a film directed by Jack Arnold (of *Creature from the Black Lagoon* fame) and variously entitled *Man in the Shadow* or *Pay the Devil*. This was quick and easy, and was produced by a character who rather amused Welles, the faintly disreputable Al Zugsmith, who had graduated (but only just) from poverty row cheapies and was later to become producer/director of unabashed pornography like *Two Roses and a Goldenrod*. However, during *Pay the Devil* Welles was up to his old tricks, rewriting the script and 'advising' the director, but for once no one seemed to care very much. And then, just when Welles least expected it, he got another offer from Zugsmith, this time not only to act, but to write and direct.

It did not start out that way: first of all he was just offered, and accepted, the role of Quinlan, a corrupt cop, in a fairly routine thriller called *Badge of Evil*. But then Charlton Heston was offered the role of the good cop, accepted it mainly in order to work with Welles, whom he revered, and 'suggested', with all the weight a big box-office star could bring to bear, that Welles direct the film too. But no matter how it came about, there the offer was. Orson Welles was back at last where he belonged, making his own movie in the heart of Hollywood.

The youngest
grand old
man

6

BADGE OF EVIL – OR *TOUCH OF EVIL*, AS IT WAS SOON
retitled – certainly was an opportunity, at just
the time Welles most needed it. And did he
make a mess of things, as he had so often
before? The answer, inevitably, is yes and no.
The 'no' part is evident for all to see in the
finished film, a masterpiece for which Welles,
whatever he may have said about it before and
after, was perfectly happy to take credit when
it won the main prize at the film festival
attached to the Brussels World's Fair in 1958.
The 'yes' part goes deeper, and concerns, as in
the case of *Macbeth*, not so much what he did
during the shooting, which went off very efficiently, to schedule, between February and
April 1957, and brought the studio some little
unexpected bonuses, without extra cost, like
the unforgettable presence of Marlene Dietrich
(who revered Welles, and did the film as a
favour to him) in the closing reels, but what
he did and did not do afterwards.

For Welles, as so often, had other fish to fry
– too many of them to make sure than any one
of them was done to a turn. He was perfectly
aware that he had taken Whit Masterson's conventional melodrama of crime and retribution
and turned it into something more complex
and involuted than his producers had ever
dreamed of. But for once he had stuck to the
limitations of time and money imposed on him,
and had given them something much more
classy and expensive-looking than they could
possibly have expected. And there were no
secrets: they had seemed delighted with what
they had seen. He had filled every corner with
telling detail, got excellent performances out of
the three principals, Charlton Heston, Janet
Leigh and himself, and brought in old allies
and friends who did it just for his sake, like
Dietrich, Mercedes McCambridge and Zsa Zsa
Gabor, to add a bit of extra spice. He had even
had an editor to work for him after shooting
was completed, Virgil Vogel (director on his
own account of *The Mole People* and other
low-budget classics), with whom he hit it off
perfectly, and had prepared most of the rough

cut that way. Maybe it was taking a little longer
than usual, and maybe he should not have
absolutely refused the front office a further
peek at the film until it was finished, but by and
large everything was going according to plan,
and perfectly in order.

But then Welles had to do a Steve Allen show
in New York, and as soon as he had gone a
screening was arranged behind his back. Welles
got that cancelled by making a scene, but lost
his editor in the process, and was advised to
stay away while the new editor completed the
job. Then things began to go sour. He was
ordered to stop in the middle of some small
retakes he was doing or at least delay them, and
regarded this as a deliberate affront. But if he
had stayed around it could surely all have been
sorted out. If he had stayed around *The Magnificent Ambersons* could have been sorted out,
Macbeth could have been sorted out. But he
had arranged to go to Mexico to do some
shooting on his television *Don Quixote*, which
had now swollen to a three-episode cinema feature, and was not to be prevented. Even
Charlton Heston, who admired Welles greatly
as actor, director and writer, could not fully
understand his behaviour. He commented:
'There's a kind of maverick streak in Orson . . .
he just wants to work, but at the same time,
there's something in him that drives him to
alienate the people with the money.'

This was where he really lost control of
Touch of Evil – and gained nothing tangible in
return, as *Don Quixote* was still lying around
incomplete at the time of his death, apparently
just another one of 'Orson's follies'. When the
studio heads finally saw *Touch of Evil* they were
unhappy. Oh, it had wonderful things in it of
course (they were delighted to have Dietrich
and wanted to credit her, but she said she
would only work for nothing with no credit.
If they wanted to give her star billing, they
could see her agent), and it had kept a big star
(Heston) happy. But wasn't it, well, a bit difficult to follow? Wouldn't ordinary movie-goers
keep worrying about where they were and who

Welles's return as a director, *Touch of Evil*, was more or less the inspiration of the moment; he was originally intended only to act in it. But the enthusiasm of co-star Charlton Heston got him the job, and his fame and wide range of friendships brought in some unexpected bonuses. Such as Marlene Dietrich in a small but key role. (She is seen below in character as the gypsy fortune-teller, and off set as her usual glamorous self.) The other actors glimpsed in these scenes from the film are Janet Leigh and Akim Tamiroff. You have only to look at Welles in makeup as the corrupt sheriff Quinlan to know that he must come to a sticky end – and so he does (bottom right).

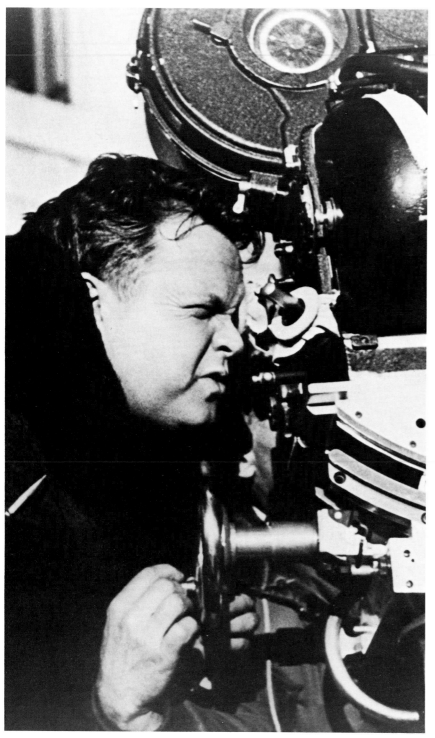

was who and what precisely was meant to be happening, buried there in Wellesian chiaroscuro? So they ordered, as they would with any ordinary studio production, some editorial clarification and the retaking or addition of brief explanatory scenes. By the time Welles was back from Mexico the first half of the film had been recut, though his version had been preserved for him to compare (and presumably argue points if he wished). Perversely, he persisted in behaving like a wounded elephant, repelling any attempts to reconcile him to some of the changes and get him to work again on completing the film. In any case he had another acting job in the works, playing the 'Big Daddy' character in Martin Ritt's Faulkner film *The Long Hot Summer*, which was being shot in Louisiana, so off he went again for another three vital months.

He should have known – he did know – better. But it almost looked like another variation on the fear-to-complete syndrome: if he virtually forced *them* to take a film out of his hands, he could then surely not be blamed if it failed . . . A last, belated attempt to shoot any retakes still needing himself came to nothing:

the studio, accused of being malicious and vengeful for so long, had actually become so. When he set off back (back home?) to Europe at New Year 1957, his much-vaunted Hollywood come-back was clearly over, leaving in its wake only bitterness and dissatisfaction on both sides. This time probably even he could not help wondering if he was really finished.

Not, of course, as an actor – he was a big and colourful enough personality always to be in demand to give a bit of his own abundant life to lifeless roles in dud pictures. His old friendship with Darryl Zanuck brought him some of the classier jobs he got in that line, taking him from harrowing African locations in John Huston's *Roots of Heaven*, next to the drunken wreck of Errol Flynn, to Hollywood again playing, in effect, the great defence lawyer Clarence Darrow in Richard Fleischer's *Compulsion*, a more-than respectable fictionalization of the notorious Leopold and Loeb murder case. He was under Fleischer's direction again the next year, this time in Paris, playing an unconvincing double role in the odd psychological drama *Crack in the Mirror*, and in between he worked briefly in France with another great, fated, self-destructive filmmaker, Abel Gance, of *Napoléon* fame, playing Fulton in his widescreen, talkie, colour follow-up *Austerlitz*. On and off he tried to get *Don Quixote* off the ground again, and began but then abandoned a television documentary about Gina Lollobrigida, of all unlikely people. But could one seriously suppose he would ever direct another movie?

But Welles was not a person you could ever safely write off: he might be a quiescent volcano, but he was far from extinct. For one thing there were so many loose ends in his life, bungled or unfinished jobs that he always wanted to have one more go at tying up better. From one viewpoint it can seem rather pathetic, this constant harking back to ideas he had first experimented with in his early radio days, or even before that, at school – rather as though he had never had a totally new idea or

Welles in a further collaboration with John Huston, *The Roots of Heaven*, as one of a group of refugees from Hemingway stuck in the African bush.

experience since *Citizen Kane*. From another
there is certainly something admirable about
the old dog's stubbornness in persistently
attempting to perfect old tricks before taking
on any new. The old trick Welles's mind
reverted to at this low point in his creative life
was none other than *Five Kings*, which he had
first tried at his Todd School graduation, and
again after the collapse of the Mercury Theatre
following *Danton's Death*. Now a visit by
Hilton Edwards in Paris sparked him into
action on the subject again. He thought he
could see, this time, just how to do it, and when
Edwards suggested that he should perfect his
text and then run it on stage with a week in
Belfast and a week in Dublin, after which, who
knows, London, New York, the World . . . he
was more than ready to listen.

What had been wrong, he decided, with even
the most trimmed-down version of the text
before, was that it had attempted to take too
much in. This time he would eliminate the sec-
tions from *Henry V*, and concentrate firmly on
the central matter of interest to him, the relationship between Falstaff and Prince Hal from
the two parts of *Henry IV*. The result he

decided to call *Chimes at Midnight*. Had he considered his latest choices in the light of that psychology he affected to despise, he would no doubt have seen their rightness for him, especially now that he was tailoring the role of Falstaff for himself and vice versa.

The crucial relationship between an ambitious, undisciplined younger man and his mentor had been constantly of importance to him in his early life: with his father, with Dadda Bernstein (whose recent death he was still mourning), with Skipper Hill, with John Houseman, with Hilton Edwards. And latterly he had tended to move himself into the other role, the wise/disreputable older man that young men could worship and emulate. But of course the relationship, viewed from either end, is liable to be troubled and shifting. Falstaff is finally rejected; Prince Hal has to reject him if he is to become a King. And Welles himself was beginning to feel like the world's rejected guest: so many friends who had now turned into enemies, so many great initiatives misunderstood and ruined. His Falstaff is not a jolly figure: the whole interpretation is, as it were, from the rejection backwards, it is haunted by the inevitability of rejection. It all makes perfect sense, if cutting down a bit on Shakespeare's original complexity (Welles in his theatrical heyday was always good at editing the complex and ambiguous into the striking and clear-cut). But he was wrong in thinking that this was the sort of Falstaff theatre audiences wanted.

The show opened in Belfast, with Keith Baxter as Prince Hal, and did respectably, if no more. Dublin was felt to be the test – Dublin where he had made his first professional stage appearance some twenty-five years before. And in Dublin the whole thing fell flat on its face. Lukewarm reviews, none of his old friends back-stage to see him after the chilly first night, and virtually no one in the audiences thereafter, even when Welles went so far to fit in with their tastes (he claimed) as to do readings of Synge to them from the stage. He had his

excuses: his wife had made some tactless remark about Irish standards of cleanliness, and so they all hated him and boycotted his work. Well, it couldn't be anything to do with the work itself, now could it? Nor, of course, could the undistinguished effect of his next theatrical work, which followed immediately, his direction of Laurence Olivier in the London premiere of Ionesco's Paris hit *Rhinoceros*. True, he did decide early on that he hated the play and thought it worthless, but he soldiered on for Larry's sake, not realizing that Larry had (like such an extraordinary number of other people he had worked with) this totally inexplicable compulsion to destroy him. True, he did leave the rehearsals four days before the opening, but that was only because Olivier told him to, and if he did not go back afterwards it was just because he was too hurt and humiliated . . .

It was probably the nasty taste this experience left following immediately on his

Dublin disaster with *Chimes at Midnight*, which further ensured that these would be his last serious attempts to work in the theatre. From this point on, he seems to have accepted his role as a wanderer and outsider from normal show-business: he was now sure that if he wanted to do anything more than coast through life on being constantly in demand for his acting, his personality or at least his name in any number of mostly worthless films – and he was unlikely to do that, since the urge to create could not be stilled – then he had to do it all himself. No one was likely to invite him to make a film of his own, or help him much towards doing so: the world seemed to be fuller and fuller of the motivelessly malignant and of friends unaccountably turned enemies. But to his credit he continued amazingly willing to take on the world; he was never resigned to exclusion and inactivity. And if he was going to fight, he had picked up enough useful hints along the way: he knew how to deal with defaulting money-men, to recognize the right moment to cut and run, to indulge champagne tastes with beer money, above all to put on a show.

In this frame of mind, he must have been very surprised to receive almost at once an actual unsolicited proposal from a real live film producer. Not perhaps the most stable and reliable of film producers, but after all, an offer was an offer. For obscure business reasons of their own, Alexander and Michel Salkind, Paris-based independents, wanted Welles to make a film of any out-of-copyright classic he cared to choose, they wanted it to be shot in Yugoslavia, and they wanted it quickly. Presumably they had some kind of deal going with the Yugoslav government, and the quicker they could get some relatively inexpensive co-production under way the better: on the other hand, their admiration for Welles and desire to work with him must have been genuine enough – otherwise why would they have picked him of all possibly available film-makers?

Welles perused the list of non-copyright possibles they sent him, and decided that the only one he was remotely interested in was Kafka's *The Trial*; though he had never found Kafka much to his taste, this was at least something he could take as a starting-point. He made an adaptation of Kafka's gloomy, dead-pan fable in double-quick time, and got together a cast headed by Anthony Perkins as K, Kafka's mysteriously threatened, almost anonymous hero, with himself in support as K's elusive advocate, Akim Tamiroff and a selection of friendly ladies more than happy to work with Welles on any terms: Jeanne Moreau, Romy Schneider, Elsa Martinelli, Susanne Flon and Katina Paxinou (whose scenes were doomed this time to end on the cutting-room floor). Welles's drawing power for actors never faded. Anthony Perkins described him as having: '... a field-marshal's affection for the troops – the crew, the actors, the extras. He's a wonderful manipulator – and I mean that in the best sense – of people and their soft spots and the ways to get them behind his vision of things.'

He began shooting exterior scenes in Zagreb, whose run-down, East European look seemed ideal for Kafka's grim world, towards the end of March 1962. Then, unpredictably (or anyway unpredicted), word came from Paris that the Salkinds had run out of money, and so could not come up with the part of the budget the Yugoslavians had agreed to match. So, no sets were being constructed in the Zagreb studios, no pay was forthcoming for the cast and crew, and the only thing to do, according to the Salkinds, was to abandon production.

They had, of course, underestimated their man: Welles was all too used to shooting with no money at all, whenever and wherever he could. The answer to their dilemma, he at once recognized, was a moonlight flit back to Paris. Once there, it should not be too impossible to improvise. And improvise he did: unable to afford studio space, let alone the sets he had designed, he had the inspiration to move into

129

Welles chose to film Kafka's novel *The Trial*, as the best of a job lot of projects offered to him. He plays a small role in it as a lawyer the ill-fated hero meets, and there are other stars in similarly episodic roles, but the main weight of the film falls on Anthony Perkins as Kafka's 'faceless' hero K, hopelessly at odds with the system. Opposite right: Welles edits the film.

the grand, abandoned Gare d'Orsay on the Left Bank, which was eventually fated to be transformed into the Musée d'Orsay. Here nooks and crannies up in the roof or down in the depths could be turned with minimal expense into the hallucinatory *terrain vague* K inhabited. Working at fever pitch, Welles had the shooting finished by 2 June, in under nine weeks. He was then able to edit the film just as he wanted, and had it ready for its Paris premiere by 21 December. Circumstances might have intervened, but for once neither the malevolence of colleagues nor erratic behaviour on the part of Welles himself had ruined the enterprise.

On the other hand, unfortunately, *The Trial* was not a film Welles wanted to make, but only the best chance that offered. One might say the same about *Touch of Evil*, but in that case he was able to take over the material and make it his own. One would have to say, just at a glance, that the glacial, geometrical genius of Kafka and the baroque elaboration of Welles must be deeply and mutually inimical – a fact that possibly Welles recognized himself. He later justified his choice, saying: 'I don't believe in an essential reverence for the original material. It's simply part of the collaboration. I felt no need to be true to Kafka in every essence.'

Hitchcock, with his black humour and his cool, level gaze, would have been the ideal film-maker to bring Kafka to the screen (it is recorded that when Kafka was reading the terrible, nihilistic last scene of *The Trial* to friends he laughed so much he fell off his chair), but trying to make Kafka over into Welles was almost certain to produce something which lost the distinctive qualities of the one without acquiring the distinctive qualities of the other. Much as Welles's admirers wanted to like *The Trial*, few of them succeeded, and by general consent it is just about his least satisfactory film.

However, it had kept him working, and picked him up when he was particularly down.

His necessarily brief stay in Yugoslavia also brought him a bonus in the shape of Oja Kodar, a Yugoslavian sculptor and writer he met in Zagreb and who was to be his constant companion and assistant for the rest of his life – though he remained married to Paola Mori and was as attentive a father to Beatrice as he had been to his other two daughters (which was not saying much, since Welles never seemed equipped by nature for parenthood, particularly perhaps of girls). He was again full of new projects: he enormously admired Joseph Heller's off-beat best-seller *Catch 22*, but failed to buy the film rights, and was finally reduced merely to acting in Mike Nichols's 1970 film of it (which he *detested*); he was supposed to be directing a segment of *The Bible*, which he scripted but then abandoned because the producers would not agree to Esau's cringing from

his father's knife; he worked on an original scenario by Oja Kodar, and another by himself about the life of Alexandre Dumas. And there was still his idea of making *Chimes at Midnight* into a film; he had it all in his mind as soon as he could set it up.

Meanwhile he was relatively inactive, even as an actor, except for appearing as a mono-maniac film director (modelled on whom? one wonders – more likely Fellini than Welles himself) filming the Crucifixion of Christ in Pier Paolo Pasolini's episode of a film initially called *RoGoPaG*, which garnered more publicity than it expected, or perhaps deserved, when it was

Chimes at Midnight, **a Falstaff film with strong autobiographical overtones. Below: Welles with Jeanne Moreau as Doll Tearsheet. Right: the missing makeup box which provided so many excuses. Below right: Welles making up as Falstaff, and the finished result.**

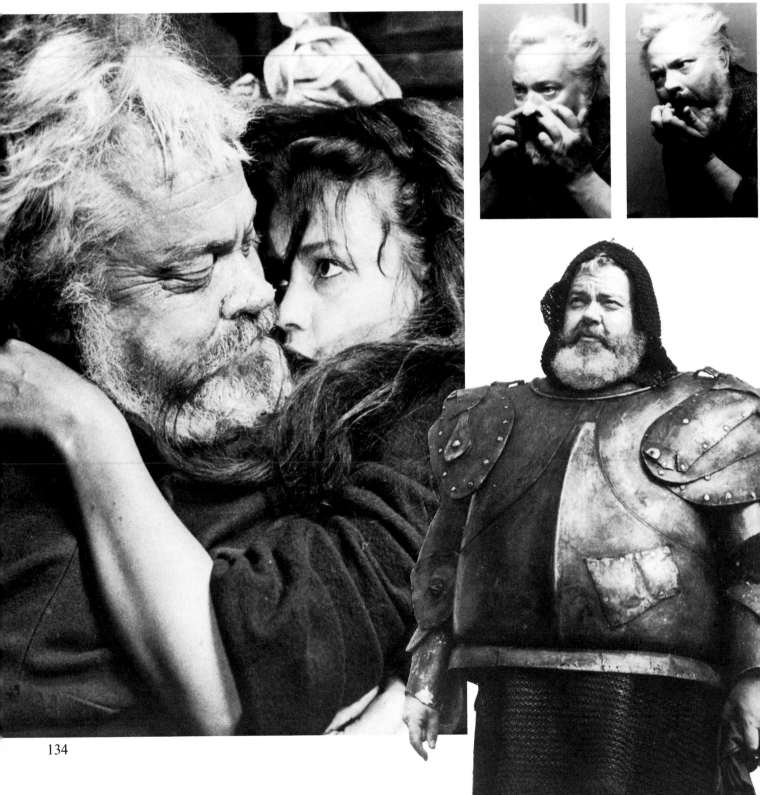

Welles and his makeshift crew filming *Chimes at Midnight*
in Spain. As usual, no detail is too small for his directorial
care and attention.

banned and the director briefly imprisoned on a charge of blasphemy. Finally, in the winter of 1964, he was able to get on with filming *Chimes at Midnight*: he had found a producer in Spain (where he had now settled, and where he stayed, until his villa just outside Madrid was badly damaged by fire in 1970), and, knowing better by now than to start out with any grandiose plans, he had in preparation cut the costs to an absolute minimum. The film was made in black-and-white, with Welles himself, of course, as Falstaff and Prince Hal played by Keith Baxter, who had played the role on stage in Ireland and though an excellent actor meant nothing at all at the film box-office, and was hence willing to work on the film very cheaply. Most of the other performers were similarly stage personalities, like the Hotspur (Norman Rodway), or Spaniards little known in the English-speaking cinema, like the Worcester (Fernando Rey, star of several Buñuel films), or stars who were also friends and admirers and did what they could in the brief periods available to them (Jeanne Moreau, John Gielgud, Margaret Rutherford). Welles became a virtuoso at making every moment of a performer's time count: as much as possible he shot on the backs of nameless Spanish stand-ins.

In a way, the film was like a home-movie: the most imposing home-movie ever made, perhaps, but still one in which audiences have often to accept the will for the deed, the spirit which informs it rather than the letter before their eyes. Welles himself was painfully aware of its technical shortcomings, but at least felt that now he had got the subject, with all its hidden autobiographical significances (intensified if anything in the time that had elapsed since the stage version), out of his system and could get on with other things. In assessing the film years later, Welles said: 'I think Shakespeare was greatly preoccupied, as I am in my humble way, with the loss of innocence, and he was profoundly against the modern age, as I am . . . I think his villains were modern people . . . and innocence is what Falstaff is . . . it's a rough

modern world he's living in. It's my favourite picture . . . it is, to me, the least flawed.'

By the time the film had its first showing at the Cannes Film Festival in 1966, out of competition, and was rapturously received, Welles was pleased enough to be honoured by a special award, but his mind was set on the future rather than harping on this part of his past.

The first thing he did after completing principal photography on *Chimes at Midnight* was not, as it happened, particularly auspicious: he began work on an adaptation of *Treasure Island*, another old favourite from Mercury Theatre on the Air days, in which he was playing his old role of Long John Silver and the direction was entrusted to Jesus Franco, the second-unit director of *Chimes at Midnight*, under, of course, Welles's close supervision. For some unexplained reason the production floundered unfinished, but Welles was not so easily put off, and reverted to the property again in 1972, when it was pushed through to completion, if not much exposure, under the direction of John Hough and Andrea Bianchi. Other acting roles were less demanding of his time and required, in a few cases, quite a bit more of his talent: in the next two or three years his appearances veered between the weird (with Jeanne Moreau in Tony Richardson's misbegotten Marguerite Duras adaptation *The Sailor from Gibraltar*) and the wonderful (his magisterial Cardinal Wolsey in Fred Zinnemann's dignified *A Man for All Seasons*), with little of import in between, though one might put in a word for his monumental Tiresias in Phillip Saville's unexpectedly interesting version of *Oedipus the King*.

As usual, these were all means to ends – the very natural, immediate end of supporting himself and his family and the more ambitious end of realizing some more of his ideas on film before he was too old, too tired or just (as his girth went gradually out of control) too fat. In 1966, when he began shooting the last completed film which was all his, *The Immortal*

Story, he was, though one forgets it, just turned fifty, no age at all for a man these days. But he had been famous for so long, for so many years the oldest *enfant terrible* out of captivity, that it was difficult now to realize that his Grand Old Man act was just an act, for he must surely be accounted the youngest Grand Old Man on the face of the earth. *The Immortal Story* itself, shot in Paris and Madrid between September and November 1966, was deliberately slight, a further exploration of the kind of territory Welles had mapped out in *The Fountain of Youth*. It was just under an hour, and was originally designed for French television, though in the event everyone was so pleased with it (and it went so far over the envisaged budget) that it had a simultaneous theatrical release in France and was shown as a short feature elsewhere.

It is based on a story by one of Welles's favourite authors, Isak Dinesen (otherwise the Baroness Blixen), about the unavailing attempt of a rich and lonely old man (Welles) to make one of the sea's famous myths into reality by paying a young sailor to spend one night of love with a barren wife and father her child. The 'wife' is actually an aging prostitute (Jeanne Moreau) and the sailor actually a Billy Budd-like angelic innocent (Norman Eshley), and the plot fails, though the encounter does not, because neither is willing to pass on the truth to others in validation of the myth: if art is to become life, it can only do so in secret, and not at the behest of a wilful outsider who wants to play God. This all sounds very like some kind of allegory of the film-making process, as seen by Welles at this late stage in his career, but it is difficult to define what it means. Probably it is a deliberate irony that what the character Welles plays in the film fails to do – make a fiction reality – is precisely what Welles the film-maker succeeds in doing by the act of making this film. If it was designed as a farewell to his art, it could hardly be more apposite as an affirmation of survival. But of course this could not be, and was not, how

Welles intended to end: it was just another 'home movie', as technically shaky as *Chimes at Midnight*, meant to keep his hand in while he prepared for the next major task.

As we now know, *The Immortal Story* was in a very real sense Welles's swansong. Exactly why is as hard as ever to pin down. Financial difficulties, of course. Sheer blind misfortune in almost unbelievable doses. Failing health. And at last death just when all three of his latest projects (or anyway surely at least one of them) seemed about to come to fruition. Yes, all of that may be true, and probably is. And yet, as with the man Welles had compared himself to who, every time he stepped out of doors, got struck by lightning, in the aggregate it seems somehow oddly unconvincing. However, this

is what seems to have happened.

Late in 1967, after a quick trip to the States and a lucrative first appearance on Dean Martin's television show, Welles began shooting his new feature, at that time called *The Deep*, off the Dalmatian coast of Yugoslavia. It was based on a thriller novel by Charles Williams called *Dead Calm*, which is a five-handed drama all taking place in one day on two boats, the ketch in which Michael Bryant and Olga Palinkas are taking their honeymoon, and the sinking yacht from which an apparently innocent stranger (Laurence Harvey) has come with tales of disaster. His story proves to be a fabrication, as the honeymoon husband finds out when he encounters the other two survivors on the yacht (Welles and Jeanne Moreau), but that leaves him with the problem of rescuing his own wife from what he now recognizes to be a madman's clutches. It all sounds fairly straightforward – disturbingly straightforward for a Welles movie – and was shot on and off in Yugoslavia throughout 1968, with Welles going off from time to time to appear in yet one more obscure Yugoslavian film to keep his own film going. According to Jeanne Moreau and Laurence Harvey in the early 1970s, it was completed according to plan, and they were just waiting for Welles's call to do anything that needed doing on the soundtrack. Since when, nothing, apart from vague rumours that Welles was trying unsuccessfully to sell it to television, and later, his obscure pronouncements that he thought it was dated and would probably emerge only as a posthumous work. Later still, Welles grew even more evasive, and alleged he had never been able to complete shooting owing to the death of Laurence Harvey (which did not, for the record, take place until October 1973).

In 1970 Welles was in any case now interested in pursuing another project. In collaboration with Oja Kodar he reworked an old script of his called *The Sacred Beasts*, a satirical tale of a washed-up Hollywood director living it up in Spain, which in its turn went back to his novel *Une Grosse Légume*, which went back to his 1950 play *The Unthinking Lobster*. The new version was called *The Other Side of the Wind*, and the locale was moved back to Hollywood itself. Unable to attract any Hollywood (or even television) money, Welles began, yet again, shooting with his own money in California that August. What he was then shooting, it subsequently emerged, was something which would eventually be a movie within the movie: his old director's attempt, disastrous we presume, to be up-to-the-minute. He said he had made the whole thing, but would be using only about half of it in *The Other Side of the Wind*.

Then an avenging angel, in the shape of the American tax authorities, descended on him, querying his tax-residence in Switzerland and demanding vast amounts of back taxes. Welles retreated to Europe and looked for some way of making money fast. Hence *F for Fake*, his official last completed movie. Somehow he came across a half-hour television documentary shot by French film-maker François Reichenbach a few years before about the famous art-forger Elmyr de Hory, at that time living in comfortable retirement in Ibiza. Among the people featured in the Reichenbach film was a journalist called Clifford Irving, who was then writing a book about de Hory, and had some very interesting things to say about forgery, its motives and psychology. Meanwhile, of course, Irving himself had become notorious with his own ambitious forgery, the supposed autobiography of the long-unseen Howard Hughes. Seizing on this ironic hindsight, Welles saw a way to re-edit the Reichenbach material with added comment of his own to make a short semi-documentary feature out of it, primarily for television. And in his hands it grew into a meditation on the whole question of the faker as artist and the artist as faker – de Hory, Irving and himself. Then he had the inspiration to tag on a short story about a girl played by Oja Kodar who plays a little trick on Picasso which is not quite

140

Welles directing John Huston (instead of vice versa) in his last, unfinished film, *The Other Side of the Wind*, **in which Huston plays an old film-maker as refracted in the films and videos, movie nuts from all over the world make to celebrate his birthday.**

what it seems. And is it true? We might ask Welles at the end. He has his answer: 'I did promise, that for one hour I would tell you only the truth. That hour, ladies and gentlemen, is over. For the last seventeen minutes, I've been lying my head off.'

Though the film is obviously thin, spinning out its material rather further than it will comfortably go, and is a credit to Welles's editing skills rather than his directing, it does represent as perhaps nothing else he did on screen the maddening charm of the man, the reason that people who had surely been punished enough kept coming back for more. It was a little success, but a success all the same. And with the money from that, and from acting in some even sillier films than usual, including two by the 'king of the Z's', Bert I. Gordon (*The Toy Factory* and *Necromancy*), Welles was able to contemplate going back to work on *The Other Side of the Wind*, after a hiatus of nearly two years.

After this, events become confusing. He had found, it seemed, a Spanish backer, and then an Iranian group ready to match him dollar for dollar – plus a Paris-based, Iranian-financed production company. From the tale of international skulduggery which follows we need only note that the Spaniard was a confidence trickster, diverting into his own pocket funds provided for Welles by the Iranians, and that even when he was exposed the fall of the Shah and

the advent of the Ayatollah made all reasonable dealing with the Iranians impossible. Or so Welles claimed, and there seems no reason to disbelieve him. While all this was happening, he was happily shooting away in California with his cast of celebrities at a script which had, not quite surprisingly, become *Chimes at Midnight* over again, with John Huston as the disreputable old film-maker and mentor of the young intellectual (Peter Bogdanovich) who is eventually bound to reject and betray him. Among the others to be glimpsed were the French director Claude Chabrol (in whose film *La Décade Prodigieuse* Welles had just appeared), Susan Strasberg (playing a sort of Pauline Kael-figure, in retaliation no doubt for Kael's down-grading of Welles in *The Citizen Kane Book*) and old Mercury Theatre survivors like Paul Stewart, Mercedes McCambridge and Norman Foster. In February 1975 Welles was honoured by the American Film Institute with its lifetime-achievement trophy, and showed two edited sequences from the film-in-progress. That was the last anyone saw of it, for shortly afterwards the frantic Iranians impounded all the material (completely or almost completely shot as it was) and refused to let Welles get his hands on it ever again. So, as far as we know, he never did, and that was the end of that project.

During the last ten years of his life Welles acted little on the large screen – his health increasingly forbade it – and not at all on stage. He mellowed with the years, giving a wonderfully relaxed and warm-hearted vision of himself in Leslie Megahy's definitive 1982 television interview, and even effusively making up with his old, alleged 'enemy' John Houseman, before millions on the Merv Griffin chat show, describing him as 'the closest friend I've ever had'.

He found a significant new source of income using his still splendid, unmistakable voice for television commercials, to impart a desirable touch of class: if you heard Welles telling you how good Paul Masson wines or frozen peas

from Britain or definitely non-Havana cigars were, how could you fail to believe him? And he went on inventing films in his mind, supported now by the adoration of a whole new generation of Hollywood film-makers who had grown up in his giant shadow. The most practical of these was Henry Jaglom, in whose whimsical fantasy *A Safe Place* Welles had played in 1971. Jaglom tried to get another Welles adaptation from Isak Dinesen, *The Dreamers*, into production, without success. He bullied Welles into writing a new original, *The Big Brass Ring*, which was another variation on the Falstaff / Prince Hal relationship, this time apparently given a specifically homosexual twist. No one was interested in that either. In 1983 Welles was all fired up again about filming his *King Lear*, now that he was finally the right age, and was even willing to consider a tentative approach from Alexander Salkind, whom he had hardly seen since *The Trial*. Salkind suggested a sort of trade-off: Welles would play

a small role in Salkind's new extravaganza *Where is Parsifal?* and he would try to come up with money for *Lear*. But then his production of *Superman III* had done badly at the box-office (who would have expected it, after the success of *Superman I* and *II*?) so there was no knowing when or whether he would manage it.

On 6 May 1985 Welles was inevitably in the news: it was, after all, at long last, his seventieth birthday. On British television the marathon two-part interview he had done with Leslie Megahey in 1982 was repeated, showing him at his most lively, charming and disarming. And there seemed at last to be good news. Jaglom was in high hopes that *The Dreamers* would really happen. Salkind might finally have the money for *King Lear*, and if he did not, several European television companies were interested. Since Welles had just managed to get the French courts to recognize his legal ownership of *The Other Side of the Wind* material (which he now confusingly described as 'supposedly a collection of 35mm, 16mm, 8mm and video tape films, made by cinema nuts from all over the world who are gathered for the birthday of an old director . . . Nothing in it is as seen by me . . .'), he might get to complete that, if he could work on it, as the courts required, in Paris. And there was something completely new on the horizon as well: a film of and about the first night of *The Cradle Will Rock*, originally devised by a young film-maker called Michael Fitzgerald but taken over and reworked by Welles himself. Finance? Well, it had been backed by Universal (budget $5½ million), but then they had changed their mind. However, it *will* be made, said Fitzgerald.

None of it happened, and by early October Welles was found dead in his Los Angeles home. Alone and despairing, announced a French newspaper picturesquely, though neither appears to have been the case. He was only seventy, yet he seemed to have been there for ever. What would you expect, if you had made the greatest film in the history of the cinema when you were only twenty-five?

143

*The man
and the
myth*

7

PICTURE, IF YOU WILL, THE NOSE. OR IF YOU *CAN*, for Welles seldom appeared on stage or screen for two occasions with the same nose. He even, once, changed noses in mid-film. His obsession, unrealized, with playing Cyrano de Bergerac, which he pursued with some determination through at least half his career, no doubt had something to do with the actor craving the plum role, but even more it must have had to do with some persistent dissatisfaction with his own nose – too small and cute, he thought, for the rest of his increasingly imposing frame. But the preoccupation with noses in its turn must have been an excuse, a focus for Welles's lifelong passion for disguise. Not, evidently, such a rare passion in an actor. There are some famous ones, like Welles's old friend and antagonist Laurence Olivier, who are most truly alive when covered with padding and false hair. Others find physical, and especially facial, disguise an inhibiting factor: Dirk Bogarde, for instance, could not function at all as Von Aschenbach in *Death in Venice* until he took off the false nose Visconti had insisted on to make him look more like Mahler. Welles would have loved it.

But it was not only in his visible professional life that Welles craved disguise. He was a master of illusion and loved to demonstrate the fact. The creator – by which he meant primarily himself – is an illusionist, making us believe, or at least half-believe, things that are not so. Of course we know that the lady in spangles on the stage has not really just been sawn in half, just as we know that however unstoppably that express-train may be bearing down on her, the heroine of the movie is not going to be minced up in the first reel, or even the last. But in the excitement of the moment, we can suspend disbelief, accept illusion for reality, conspire to forget what we know perfectly well to be so. We can let ourselves be manipulated, and that is what Welles loved to prove, over and over again.

It may be the manoeuvre of a very insecure man, desperate to impose order on a hostile and unmanageable world. That is surely what that other great Hollywood illusionist, Alfred Hitchcock, was, and why he made films the way he did. With Welles it is difficult to feel so sure. They say that every extreme has buried within it its own opposite, struggling to get out: each bully is a coward at heart, each braggart a shrinking violet, each compulsive womanizer a homosexual . . . Well, maybe, but it is difficult to imagine Orson Welles in that trembling moment before he was confident. The earliest outside testimonies we have of him – and they are very early indeed – all agree that his great advantage was his real, unshakable confidence in himself, and the fact that he was a genius. If there was any doubt in his mind when he was sixteen, the sharp, malicious eye of Micheal MacLiammoir failed completely to detect it.

Doubts must have come later. Goethe said that there is only one thing worse than not having your wish granted, and that is having it granted. Welles had all his important wishes granted by the time he was twenty-six, and spent most of his subsequent life wishing he had framed them better. Practically everything he had tried to do at school, or tried out on The Mercury Theatre on the Air, he was still worrying away at fifty years later, hoping that this time he would be able to do it completely right. And fearing, of course, that he would not, and the world would tell him so. Fear not to start; fear to complete: between these two poles his life was lived. He had more than his share of luck: good luck and bad. He had and lost more of almost everything than any ordinary man ever comes within sight of. Any complete view of him must be what Richard Aldington called his biography of D. H. Lawrence: *Portrait of a Genius But . . .*

Genius there can be no doubt Welles was, even if, sometimes unbecomingly, he knew it. At the very least, *Citizen Kane*, *The Magnificent Ambersons*, *Othello* and *Touch of Evil* are magic, unforgettable films. Many talented film-makers who fill a long professional life with activity do not manage a quarter as much.

Welles the director in action. Opposite, on *Citizen Kane,*
above, on *The Lady from Shanghai*; **right, on** *It's All True*.

His theatre work is, in the nature of things, more difficult to assess at this distance of time, for people who were not there and can judge only by the report of others. I can say that his *Moby Dick* was one of the most amazing, wonderful, mysterious evenings I have ever spent in the theatre: only on perhaps two or three other occasions in the theatre have I had such a sense of being in the presence of a director of genius, shaping everything just the way he wanted and holding the audience in the palm of his hand. I can therefore understand when people report the same of his best Mercury Theatre productions, but there is no way I or any of us can substantiate what they say.

As a writer and designer he had a certain skill, though nothing exceptional. As an actor . . . Now there is a problem. Of course he was forceful, bursting with a personality which he could not suppress even if he would – as many makers of negligible films found out to their cost (in shattered nerves) and their advantage (in the curiously transfigured results of their labours). That he was quite what you would call a great actor remains problematic: for all his false noses, he was always essentially himself, or some aspect of his fantasy of himself. But since with Walt Whitman, whose *A Song of Myself* he so beautifully read for BBC radio, he could reasonably say, 'I am vast. I comprehend multitudes', no one was likely to complain of monotony in the performance. And no actor could do more with less: everyone remembers him first when thinking of *The Third Man*, which so oddly mirrors the structure of his favourite Conrad *The Heart of Darkness*, even though like the legendary Kurtz when finally run to earth, he has really only one scene and has to create his effect entirely by force of personality, the kind of instant authority which brooks no denial.

It is hard to say how seriously Welles took himself specifically as an actor – it is hard to say how seriously he took himself specifically as anything. He must have taken himself seriously as a film-maker, otherwise he would not have gone on endlessly fighting to set up yet another production, each time against all the odds. As noted, he himself said in later life that he thought *Moby Dick – Rehearsed* was very likely the best thing he ever did in any medium – but then there may have been an element of tease even in that. Certainly he wanted desperately to be taken seriously as a director, in the theatre and the cinema, and one suspects that that was partially the reason for such mis-

Welles playing movie-men. Above: as the advertising director in *I'll Never Forget What's-'is-Name*. **Opposite: as the monomaniac director in** *RoGoPaG*.

fires as *Mr Arkadin* and *The Trial*, as well as possibly his coyness about *The Deep*. His Achilles heel, and the only area where he seems to have been consistently taken in himself, was his infatuation, not unknown in other American artists, or indeed in people anywhere with some doubt about the thoroughness of their education, with this idea of intellectualism, the whole schmeer of supposed European subtlety, sophistication and complexity. He was funda-

mentally a small-town boy, very quick and bright rather than deep, who had a brilliant instinct for showmanship and a grasp of the bare bones of any subject which could have made him a great popularizer – and, in his early Mercury stage productions, did. If only he had not wanted so much the regard of the intellectuals as well as the applause of the crowd . . . But then again, he was likely to be carried beyond comprehension as much by his own ebullience and inventiveness, as by mere pretension and eagerness to pass himself off, even to himself, as something other than he was.

So was Welles ultimately a faker, as he implies in *F for Fake*, ranging himself in the same gallery as Elmyr de Hory and Clifford Irving? Clearly that is how, in some moods at least, he saw himself – though he would surely have added that it was no discreditable thing. After all, is not every artist a bit of a showman, and every showman a bit of a fake? Of all the images of himself he toyed with, all the personalities he presented to the public, this was the most persistent, and if it began as a mask, perhaps eventually he grew into it. But if he was an illusionist by vocation, he was not a dishonest illusionist: he laid all his cards on the table, and only then started slipping them up his sleeve. And his best trick of all was that, at the end of the day, he really did deliver what he was pretending to deliver. We can mourn forever the loss of all his might-have-beens. But that cannot finally prevent us from cherishing and revering a handful of films which will continue to captivate and amaze as long as celluloid or video holds together. Orson Welles was his own creation (with God as associate producer), and no doubt on his seventh anniversary as on his seventieth, he beheld what he had wrought and was, by and large, satisfied.

Perhaps we should leave the last word with the actress Jeanne Moreau. 'For me he is a destitute king. Destitute not because he was thrown away from the kingdom, but because on this earth, there is no kingdom that is good enough for Orson Welles.'

Bibliography

Maurice Bessy: *Orson Welles*. Paris 1970

Roger Carringer: *The Making of Citizen Kane*. Berkeley 1985

Jean Cocteau, André Bazin: *Orson Welles*. Paris 1950

Peter Cowie: *A Ribbon of Dreams: The Cinema of Orson Welles*. London 1973

Richard France: *The Theatre of Orson Welles*. Lewisburg 1977

Ronald Gottesman (editor): *Focus on Citizen Kane*. Englewood Cliffs 1971. *Focus on Orson Welles*. Englewood Cliffs 1976

Charles Higham: *The Films of Orson Welles*. Berkeley 1970. *Hollywood Cameramen: Sources of Light*. London 1970. *Orson Welles*. New York 1985

John Houseman: *Run-through*. New York 1972. *Front and Center*, New York 1979. *Final Dress*. New York 1983

Pauline Kael: *The Citizen Kane Book*. Boston 1973

John Kobal: *Rita Hayworth*. London 1977

Howard Koch: *The Panic Broadcast*. New York 1970. *As Time Goes By*. New York 1979

Lawrence Langner: *The Magic Curtain*. New York 1951

Barbara Leaming: *Orson Welles*. New York 1985

Joseph McBride: *Orson Welles*. London 1972

Micheal MacLiammoir: *All for Hecuba*. London 1946. *Put Money in Thy Purse*. London 1952

Peter Meryman: *Mank: The Wit, World and Life of Herman Mankiewicz*. New York 1978

James Naremore: *The Magic World of Orson Welles*. New York 1978

Peter Noble: *The Fabulous Orson Welles*. London 1956

FILMOGRAPHY

1934

1 Hearts of Age
DIRECTORS Orson Welles, William Vance
CAST Orson Welles, Virginia Nicolson, William Vance.
RUNNING TIME 4 minutes
PRODUCED BY William Vance
(A copy of this film maybe seen in the Library of Congress Film Archives in Washington)

1941

2 Citizen Kane (Mercury Productions) ▽
DIRECTOR Orson Welles
CAST Orson Welles (Charles Foster Kane), Joseph Cotten (Jedediah Leland, also Newsreel Reporter), Everett Sloane (Bernstein), Dorothy Comingore (Susan Alexander Kane), Ray Collins (James W. Gettys), William Alland (Jerry Thompson, also Newsreel Narrator), Agnes Moorehead (Mary Kane), Ruth Warrick (Emily Norton Kane), George Goulouris (Walter Parks Thatcher), Erskine Sanford (Herbert Carter, also Newsreel Reporter), Harry Shannon (Jim Kane), Philip Van

Zandt (Rawlston), Paul Stewart (Raymond), Fortunio Bonanova (Matisti), Georgia Backus (Miss Anderson, Curator of Thatcher Library), Buddy Swan (Charles Foster Kane, aged 8), Sonny Bupp (Kane, Jr), Gus Schilling (Head Waiter), Richard Barr (Hillman), Joan Blair (Georgia), Al Eben (Mike), Charles Bennett (Entertainer), Milt Kibbee (Reporter), Tom Curran (Teddy Roosevelt), Irving Mitchel (Dr Corey), Edith Evanson (Nurse), Arthur Kay (Orchestra Leader), Tudor Williams (Chorus Master), Herbert Corthell (City Editor), Benny Rubin (Smather), Edmund Cobb (Reporter), Frances Neal (Ethel), Robert Dudley (Photographer), Ellen Lowe

(Miss Townsend), Gino Corrado (Gino, the waiter), Alan Ladd, Louise Currie, Eddie Coke, Walter Sande, Arthur O'Connell, Katherine Trosper and Richard Wilson (Reporters).
EXECUTIVE PRODUCER George J. Schaefer
SCREENPLAY Herman J. Mankiewicz, Orson Welles
PHOTOGRAPHY Gregg Toland
EDITORS Mark Robson, Robert Wise
RUNNING TIME 119 minutes
PRODUCED BY Orson Welles

1942

3 The Magnificent Ambersons (Mercury △ Productions)
DIRECTOR Orson Welles (additional scenes directed by Freddie Fleck and Robert Wise)
CAST Orson Welles (Narrator), Tim Holt (George Amberson Minafer), Joseph Cotten (Eugene Morgan), Dolores Costello (Isabel Amberson Minafer), Agnes Moorehead (Fanny Minafer), Anne Baxter (Lucy Morgan), Ray Collins (Jack Amberson), Richard Bennett (Major Amberson), Don Dillaway (Wilbur Minafer), Erskine Sanford (Roger Bronson), J. Louis Johnson (Sam), Gus Schilling (Drugstore Clerk), Charles Phipps (Uncle John), Dorothy Vaughan and Elmer Jerome (Spectators at funeral), Olive Ball (Mary), Nina Guilbert and John Elliot (Guests), Anne O'Neal (Mrs Foster), Kathryn Sheldon and Georgia Backus

(Matrons), Henry Roquemore (Hardware Man), Hilda Plowright (Nurse), Mel Ford (Fred Kinney), Bob Pittard (Charlie Johnson), Lillian Nicholson (Landlady), Billy Elmer (House Servant), Maynard Holmes and Lew Kelly (Citizens), Bobby Cooper (George as a boy), Drew Roddy (Elijah), Jack Baxley (Reverend Smith), Heenan Elliott (Labourer), Nancy Gates (Girl), John Maguire (Young Man), Ed Howard (Chauffeur/Citizen), William Blees (Youth at accident), James Westerfield (Cop at accident), Philip Morris (Cop), Jack Santoro (Barber), Louis Hayward (extra).
EXECUTIVE PRODUCER George J. Schaefer
PHOTOGRAPHY Stanley Cortez
EDITORS Robert Wise, Jack Moss, Mark Robson
RUNNING TIME 88 minutes (originally 131 minutes)
PRODUCED BY Orson Welles

1944

4 Journey into Fear (Mercury ▷ Productions)
DIRECTOR Norman Foster (and Orson Welles, uncredited)
CAST Joseph Cotten (Howard Graham), Dolores Del Rio (Josette Martel), Orson Welles (Colonel Haki), Ruth Warrick (Stephanie Graham), Agnes Moorehead (Mrs Mathews), Everett Sloane (Kopeikin), Jack Moss (Banat), Jack Durant (Gogo), Eustace Wyatt (Dr Haller), Frank Readick

(Mathews), Edgar Barrier (Kuvetli), Stefan Schnabel (Purser), Hans Conreid (Oo Lang Sang, the magician), Robert Meltzer (Steward), Richard Bennett (Ship's Captain), Shifra Haran (Mrs Haklet), Herbert Drake, Bill Roberts.
EXECUTIVE PRODUCER George J. Schaefer
SCREENPLAY Joseph Cotten, Orson Welles, based on the novel by Eric Ambler
PHOTOGRAPHY Karl Struss
EDITOR Mark Robson
RUNNING TIME 71 minutes
PRODUCED BY Orson Welles

spoof magical act in collaboration with Marlene Dietrich), Dinah Shore, Donald O'Connor and Peggy Ryan, W. C. Fields, Sophie Tucker, Arthur Rubinstein.
SCREENPLAY Lou Breslow, Gertrude Purcell
RUNNING TIME 114 minutes
PRODUCED BY Charles K. Feldman

1946

7 Tomorrow is Forever (International △ Pictures)
DIRECTOR Irving Pichel
CAST Claudette Colbert (Elizabeth Macdonald), George Brent (Larry Hamilton), Orson Welles (Erich Kessler/ John Macdonald), Natalie Wood, Richard Long.
SCREENPLAY Lenore Coffee, from the novel by Gwen Bristow
PHOTOGRAPHY Joseph Valentine
RUNNING TIME 104 minutes

8 The Stranger (International Pictures) ▽
DIRECTOR Orson Welles
CAST Orson Welles (Franz Kindler alias Professor Charles Rankin), Loretta Young (Mary Longstreet), Edward G. Robinson

1944 (re-released 1946)

5 Jane Eyre (20th Century Fox) △
DIRECTOR Robert Stevenson
CAST Orson Welles (Edward Rochester), Joan Fontaine (Jane Eyre), Margaret O'Brien (Adele Varena), Henry Daniell (Mr Brocklehurst), Peggy Ann Garner (Young Jane), Hillary Brooke (Blanche Ingram), John Sutton, Sara Allgood, Agnes Moorehead, Edith Barrett, Aubrey Mather, Barbara Everest, Ethel Griffies, Mae Marsh, Eily Malyon.

SCREENPLAY Robert Stevenson, Aldous Huxley, John Houseman, based on the novel by Charlotte Bronte
RUNNING TIME 97 minutes

6 Follow the Boys (Universal) ▽
DIRECTOR Eddie Sutherland
CAST George Raft, Vera Zorina, Charley Grapewin, Charles Butterworth, Grace MacDonald, Regis Toomey, Martha O'Driscoll, and guest stars including Jeanette McDonald, Orson Welles (in a

PHOTOGRAPHY John L. Russell
EDITOR Louis Lindsay
RUNNING TIME 107 minutes, later cut to 86 minutes
PRODUCED BY Orson Welles

1949

11 Black Magic (Edward Small ▽ Productions)
DIRECTOR Gregory Ratoff
CAST Orson Welles (Cagliostro), Nancy Guild (Marie Antoinette and Lorenza), Akim Tamiroff (Gitano), Valentina Cortese (Zoraida), Margot Grahame (Mme Du Barry), Charles Goldner (Dr Mesmer), Raymond Burr (Alexandre Dumas Jr), Frank Latimore (Gilbert), Stephen Bekassy (De Montagne)
SCREENPLAY Charles Bennett
PHOTOGRAPHY Ubaldo Arata, Anchise Brizzi
EDITORS James McKay, Fred Feitshans
RUNNING TIME 104 minutes
PRODUCED BY Gregory Ratoff

(Inspector Wilson), Philip Merivale (Judge Longstreet), Richard Long (Noah Longstreet), Byron Keith (Dr Lawrence), Billy House (Mr Potter), Martha Wentworth (Sarah), Konstantin Shayne (Konrad Meinike), Theodore Gottlieb (Farbright), Pietro Sosso (Mr Peabody), Isabel O'Madigan.
SCREENPLAY Anthony Veiller (and John Huston, Orson Welles, uncredited) based on a story by Victor Trivas, Decla Dunning
PHOTOGRAPHY Russell Metty
EDITOR Ernest Nims
RUNNING TIME 95 minutes (85 minutes in US, originally 155 minutes)
PRODUCED BY S. P. Eagle (Sam Spiegel)

9 The Lady from Shanghai (Columbia) △
DIRECTOR Orson Welles
CAST Orson Welles (Michael O'Hara), Rita Hayworth (Elsa Bannister), Everett Sloane (Arthur Bannister), Glenn Anders (George Grisby), Ted De Corsia (Sidney Broom), Gus Schilling (Goldie), Louis Merrill (Jake), Erskine Sanford (Judge), Carl Frank (District Attorney Galloway), Evelyn Ellis (Bessie), Wong Show Chong (Li), Harry Shannon (Horse cab driver), Sam Nelso (Captain), Richard Wilson (District Attorney's Assistant), and players of the Mandarin Theatre of San Francisco.
EXECUTIVE PRODUCER Harry Cohn
SCREENPLAY Orson Welles, freely adapted from the novel *If I Die Before I Wake* by Sherwood King
PHOTOGRAPHY Charles Lawton Jr
EDITOR Viola Lawrence
RUNNING TIME 86 minutes

1948

10 Macbeth (Mercury Productions for ▷ Republic Pictures)
DIRECTOR Orson Welles
CAST Orson Welles (Macbeth), Jeanette Nolan (Lady Macbeth), Dan O'Herlihy

(Macduff), Edgar Barrier (Banquo), Roddy McDowall (Malcolm), Erskine Sanford (Duncan), Alan Napier (A Holy Father), John Dierkes (Ross), Keene Curtis (Lennox), Peggy Webber (Lady Macduff/ Witch), Lionel Braham (Siward), Archie Heugly (Young Siward), Christopher Welles (Macduff child), Brainerd Duffield (1st Murderer/Witch), William Alland (2nd Murderer), George Chirello (Seyton), Gus Schilling (Porter), Jerry Farber (Fleance), Lurene Tuttle (Gentlewoman/Witch), Charles Lederer (Witch), Robert Alan (3rd Murderer), Morgan Farley (Doctor).
EXECUTIVE PRODUCER Charles K. Feldman
SCREENPLAY Orson Welles, adapted from the play by Shakespeare

156

12 Prince of Foxes (20th Century Fox) △
DIRECTOR Henry King
CAST Tyrone Power (Orsini), Orson Welles
(Cesare Borgia), Wanda Hendrix (Camilla),
Felix Aylmer (Varano), Everett Sloane
(Belli), Katina Paxinou (Mona Zoppo),
Marina Berti (Angela), Leslie Bradley
(Esteban).
SCREENPLAY Milton Krims, from the novel
by Samuel Shellabarger
PHOTOGRAPHY Leon Shamroy
EDITOR Barbara McLean
RUNNING TIME 107 minutes
PRODUCED BY Sol C. Siegel

13 The Third Man (London Films) ▽
DIRECTOR Carol Reed
CAST Joseph Cotten (Martins), Trevor
Howard (Calloway), Valli (Anna), Orson
Welles (Lime), Bernard Lee (Sgt Paine),
Paul Hoebiger (Porter), Ernst Deutsch
(Kurtz), Siegfried Breuer (Popescu), Erich
Ponto (Dr Winkel), Wilfrid Hyde-White
(Crabbin)
SCREENPLAY Graham Greene, from his own
unpublished story
PHOTOGRAPHY Robert Krasker, with
additional photography by John Wilcox,
Stan Pavey
EDITOR Oswald Hafenrichter
RUNNING TIME 93 minutes
PRODUCED BY Carol Reed

1950

14 The Black Rose (20th Century Fox) △
DIRECTOR Henry Hathaway
CAST Tyrone Power (Walter of Gurnie),
Orson Welles (Bayan), Jack Hawkins
(Tristram, The Bowman), Cecile Aubry
(Maryam, the Black Rose), Finlay Currie
(Alfgar), Henry Oscar (Friar Roger Bacon).
SCREENPLAY Talbot Jennings, from the
novel by Thomas B. Costain
PHOTOGRAPHY Jack Cardiff
EDITOR Manuel Del Campo
RUNNING TIME 121 minutes
PRODUCED BY Louis D. Lighton

1951

15 Return to Glennascaul (Dublin Gate
Theatre, a Micheal MacLiammoir-Hilton
Edwards Production)
DIRECTOR Hilton Edwards
CAST Orson Welles
SCREENPLAY Hilton Edwards
PHOTOGRAPHY George Fleischmann
RUNNING TIME 23 minutes

1952

16 Othello (Mercury Productions)
DIRECTOR Orson Welles
CAST Orson Welles (Othello), Micheal
MacLiammoir (Iago), Suzanne Cloutier
(Desdemona), Robert Coote (Roderigo),
Michael Lawrence (Cassio), Hilton
Edwards (Brabantio), Fay Compton
(Emilia), Nicholas Bruce (Lodovico), Jean
Davis (Montano), Doris Dowling (Bianca),
Joseph Cotten (Senator), Joan Fontaine
(Page).
SCREENPLAY Orson Welles, based on the
play by Shakespeare
PHOTOGRAPHY Anchise Brizzi, G. R. Aldo,
George Fanto, with Obadan Troiani,
Alberto Fusi
EDITORS Jean Sacha, John Shepridge, Renzo

Lucidi, William Morton
RUNNING TIME 91 minutes
PRODUCED BY Orson Welles

17 Trent's Last Case (British Lion) ▽
DIRECTOR Herbert Wilcox
CAST Orson Welles (Sigsbee Manderson),
John McCallum (John Marlowe), Miles
Malleson (Burton Cupples), Hugh
McDermott (Calvin C. Bunner), Margaret
Lockwood (Margaret Manderson), Michael
Wilding (Philip Trent).
SCREENPLAY Pamela Bower, from the novel
by E. C. Bentley

PHOTOGRAPHY Max Greene
EDITOR Bill Lewthwaite
RUNNING TIME 90 minutes
PRODUCED BY Herbert Wilcox

1953

18 L'uomo, La Bestia e la Virtu (Rosa
Films)
DIRECTOR Steno (Stefano Vanzina)
CAST 'Toto', Orson Welles (The Beast),
Celia Matania, Franca Faldini
SCREENPLAY Steno, Brancati, from the play
by Luigi Pirandello
PHOTOGRAPHY Mario Damicelli

1954

**19 Si Versailles m'était Conté △
(Versailles)** (CLM-Cocinex)
DIRECTOR Sacha Guitry
CAST Sacha Guitry (Louis XIV). Georges
Marchal (Young Louis XIV), Jean Marais
(Louis XV), Claudette Colbert (Mme de
Montespan), Micheline Presle (Mme de
Pompadour), Giselle Pascal (Louise de la
Vallière), Lana Marconi (Marie-Antoinette/
Nicole Leguay), Fernand Gravey (Molière),
Jean Desailly (Marivaux), Bernard Dhèran
(Beaumarchais), Jean-Claude Pascal (Axel
de Fersen), Orson Welles (Benjamin
Franklin), Charles Vanel (de Vergennes),
Gaby Morlay (Comtesse de la Motte), Gino
Cervi (Cagliostro), Jean-Jacques Delbo
(Comte de la Motte), Jean-Pierre Aumont
(Cardinal de Rohan), Gérard Philipe
(D'Artagnan), Jean-Louis Barrault
(Fenelon), Maurice Teynac (M de
Montespan), Edith Piaf (Une tricoteuse),
Yves Deniaud (Peasant), Jean Tissier, Pierre
Larquey, Bourvil (Museum guides), Gaston
Rey (Henry IV), Louis Arbessier (Louis
XIII), Jean-Louis Alibert (Le Vau), Pierre
Lord (Mansart), Nicole Maurey (Mme de
Fontanges), Mary Marquet (Mme de
Maintenon), Liliane Bert (Armande Béjart),
Georges Chamarat (La Fontaine), Samson
Fainsilber (Mazarin), Jeanne Boitel (Mme
de Sévigné), Olivier Mathot (Boileau),
Jacques Varennes (Colbert), Gilbert Gil
(Jean-Jacques Rousseau), Lucien Nat
(Montesquieu), Gilbert Boka (Louis XVI),
Jacques Berthier (Robespierre), Louis
Seigner (Lavoisier), René Worms
(Bassange), Jacques Morel (Böhmer),
Danièle Delorme (Louison Chabray),
Philippe Richard (Louis-Philippe), Michel

Auclair (Jacques Damiens), Brigitte Bardot
(Courtesan), Pauline Carton (A
Neighbour), Jean Chevrier (Turenne), Aimé
Clairiond (Ravarol), Nicole Courcel (Mme
de Chalis), Daniel Gélin (Jean Collinet),
Jean Murat (Louvois), Jean Richard (Du
Croisy), Tino Rossi (Gondolier), Germaine
Rouer (Mlle Moliere), Raymond Souplex
(Commissionaire) and Renée Devillers,
Claude Nollier, Paul Colline, Anny Cordy,
Duvaleix, Tania Fédor, Jacques François,
Jeanne Fusier-Gir, Constant Rémy,
Howard Vernon, Emile Drain, Gilles
Quéaunt.
SCREENPLAY Sacha Guitry
PHOTOGRAPHY Pierre Montazel
EDITOR Raymond Lamy
RUNNING TIME 158 minutes (originally 165
minutes)
PRODUCED BY Clément Duhour

20 Three Cases of Murder (Wessex, ▷
presented by London Films)
Lord Mountdrago
DIRECTOR George More O'Ferrall
CAST Orson Welles (Mountdrago), Alan
Badel (Owen), Helen Cherry (Lady
Mountdrago), Andre Morell (Dr Audlin).
SCREENPLAY Ian Dalrymple, from a story by
W. Somerset Maugham
You Killed Elizabeth
DIRECTOR David Eady
CAST Elizabeth Sellars (Elizabeth), John
Gregson (Edgar Curtain), Emrys Jones
(George Wheeler), Jack Lambert (Det-Insp
Acheson).
SCREENPLAY Sidney Carroll, from a story by
Brett Halliday
In the Picture
DIRECTOR Wendy Toye
CAST Alan Badel (Mr X), Hugh Pryse
(Jarvis), Leueen MacGrath (The Woman of
the House), Eddie Byrne (Snyder), John
Salew (Rooke).
SCREENPLAY Donald Wilson, from a story
by Roderick Wilkinson
PHOTOGRAPHY Georges Perinal
EDITOR G. Turney-Smith
RUNNING TIME 99 minutes
PRODUCED BY Ian Dalrymple, Hugh
Perceval

21 Trouble in the Glen (Republic, a ▷
Wilcox-Neagle Production)
DIRECTOR Herbert Wilcox
CAST Margaret Lockwood (Marissa), Orson
Welles (The Laird), Forrest Tucker (Lance),
Victor McLaglen (Parlan), John McCallum
(Malcolm), Eddie Byrne (Dinny Sullivan),
Archie Duncan (Nolly Dukes), Ann
Gudrun (Dandy Dinmont), Moultrie
Kelsall (Luke Carnoch), Margaret
McCourt (Alsuin), Mary Mackenzie (Kate
Carnoch)
SCREENPLAY Frank S. Nugent, from a story
by Maurice Walsh
PHOTOGRAPHY Max Greene
EDITOR Reginald Beck
RUNNING TIME 91 minutes
PRODUCED BY Herbert Wilcox

22 Napolean (Films CLM)
DIRECTOR Sacha Guitry
CAST Sacha Guitry, Michèle Morgan, Maria
Canale, Miss Darling, Gaby Morlay, M.
Bru, M. Pierry, C. Blondell, Dany Robin,
Michèle Cordoue, Flore Saint-Renaud,
Danielle Darrieux, Jeanne Boitel, Coseta
Greco, E. Rossi-Drago, Pauline Carton,
Francoise Arnoul, Silvana Pampanini,
Micheline Presle, Jeanne Fusier-Gir,
Patachou, Maria Schell, Maria Favella,
Simone Renant, Madeleine Lebeau,

Madeleine Vernet, Corinne Calvet, Lucienne Lemarchand, Lana Marconi, Carretier, Jean-Marie Robain, Paolo Stoppa, Marcel Rey, Duvaleix, Jean-Claude Pascal, Bernard Dhéran, Robert Manuel, Serge Reggiani, Pierre Brasseur, Daniel Gélin, Raymond Pellegrin, Pierre Flourens, Jean Ozenne, Jean Martinelli, Gilbert Gil, Arbessier, Jean Marchat, Marcel Trompier, Jacques Dumesnil, Claude Arlay, René Worms, Léon Walter, Luis Mariano, Marcel Vallée, Ivernel, Noël Roquevert, Roger Pigaut, Mafioli, Clariond, Vergne, Jean Degrave, Jean Chevrier, René Blancard, Marcel Raine, Martial, Jean Debucourt, Gino Cervi, Jean Paqui, Cattand, Georges Vitray, Maurice Martelier, Jean Dabet, Félix Clément, Vever, Jean Piat, Maurice Escande, Gilbert Boka, Jean Gabin, Yves Montand, Michel Nastorg, Roland Alexande, Henri Vidal, Jean Marais, Charles Moulin, Clément Duhour, Pierre Larquey, Bouvette, Raymond Bussieres, Louis de Funès, Edouard di Filippo, Pierre Mingand, Jacques Sablon, Cisse, Spanelli, A. Mestral, Maillot, Nepot, Claudy Chapeland, O. W. Fischer.
SCREENPLAY Sacha Guitry
PHOTOGRAPHY Louis Née
RUNNING TIME 190 minutes

1955

23 Mr Arkadin (UK title: **Confidential** △ **Report**) (Cervantes Film Organisation, Sevilla Studios [Spain]/Film Organisation [France]. A Mercury Production)
DIRECTOR Orson Welles
CAST Orson Welles (Gregory Arkadin),

Paola Mori (Raina Arkadin), Robert Arden (Guy Van Stratten), Akim Tamiroff (Jacob Zouk), Michael Redgrave (Burgomil Trebitsch), Patricia Medina (Mily), Mischa Auer (The Professor), Katina Paxinou (Sophie), Jack Watling (Marquis of Rutleigh), Gregoire Aslan (Bracco), Peter Van Eyck (Thaddeus), Suzanne Flon (Baroness Nagel), Tamara Shane (Woman in apartment), Frederic O'Brady (Oskar).
EXECUTIVE PRODUCER Louis Dolivet
SCREENPLAY Orson Welles, based on his own novel
PHOTOGRAPHY Jean Bourgoin
EDITOR Renzo Lucidi
RUNNING TIME 100 minutes

1956

24 Moby Dick (A Moulin Picture) ▷
DIRECTOR John Huston
CAST Gregory Peck (Captain Ahab), Richard Basehart (Ishmael), Leo Genn (Starbuck), Harry Andrews (Stubb), Bernard Miles (Manxman), Mervyn Johns (Peleg), Noel Purcell (Carpenter), Edric Connor (Daggoo), Joseph Tomelty (Peter Coffin), Philip Stainton (Bildad), Royal Dano (Elijah), Seamus Kelly (Flask), Friedrich Ledebur (Queequeg), Tamba Alleney (Pip), Orson Welles (Father Mapple), James Robertson Justice (Captain Boomer).
SCREENPLAY Ray Bradbury and John Huston, based on the novel by Herman Melville
PHOTOGRAPHY Oswald Morris
EDITOR Russell Lloyd
RUNNING TIME 115 minutes
PRODUCED BY John Huston

1957

25 Pay the Devil (US title: **Man in the** △ **Shadow**) (Albert Zugsmith Production)
DIRECTOR Jack Arnold
CAST Jeff Chandler (Ben Sadler), Orson Welles (Virgil Renchler), Colleen Miller (Skippy Renchler), Ben Alexander (Ab Begley), Barbara Lawrence (Helen Sadler), John Larch (Ed Yates), James Gleason (Hank James), Royal Dano (Aiken Clay), Paul Fix (Herb Parker), Leo Gordon (Chet Huneker), Martin Garralaga (Jesus

Cisrenos), Mario Siletti (Tony Santoro), Charles Horvath (Len Bookman), William Schalert (Jim Shaney), Joseph J. Greene (Harry Youngquist), Forrest Lewis (Jake Kelley), Harry Harvey Sr (Dr Creighton), Joe Schneider (Juan Martin), Mort Mills (Gateman).
SCREENPLAY Gene L. Coon
PHOTOGRAPHY Arthur E. Arling
EDITOR Edward Curtiss
RUNNING TIME 79 minutes
PRODUCED BY Albert Zugsmith

1958

26 Touch of Evil (Universal) △
DIRECTOR Orson Welles
CAST Orson Welles (Hank Quinlan), Charlton Heston (Ramon Miguel 'Mike' Vargas), Janet Leigh (Susan Vargas), Joseph Calleia (Pete Menzies), Akim Tamiroff ('Uncle Joe' Grande), Valentin De Vargas (Pancho), Ray Collins (District Attorney Adair), Dennis Weaver (Motel Clerk), Joanna Moore (Marcia Linnekar), Mort Mills (Schwartz), Marlene Dietrich

(Tanya), Victor Millan (Manolo Sanchez), Lalo Rios (Risto), Michael Sargent (Pretty Boy), Mercedes McCambridge (Gang Leader), Joseph Cotten (Detective), Zsa Zsa Gabor (Owner of strip joint), Phil Harvey (Blaine), Joe Lansing (Blonde), Harry Shannon (Gould), Rusty Wescoatt (Casey), Wayne Taylor, Ken Miller and Raymond Rodriguez (Gang Members), Arlene McQuade (Ginnie), Domenick Delgarde (Lackey), Joe Basulto (Young Delinquent), Jennie Dias (Jackie), Yolanda Bojorquez (Bobbie), Eleanor Dorado (Lia).
SCREENPLAY Orson Welles, freely adapted from the novel *Badge of Evil* by Whit Masterson
PHOTOGRAPHY Russell Metty
EDITORS Virgil V. Vogel, Aron Stell
RUNNING TIME 93 minutes
PRODUCED BY Albert Zugsmith

▽ **27 The Long, Hot Summer** (20th Century Fox)
DIRECTOR Martin Ritt
CAST Paul Newman (Ben Quick), Joanne Woodward (Clara Varner), Anthony Franciosa (Jody), Orson Welles (Varner), Lee Remick (Eula Varner), Angela Lansbury (Minnie), Richard Anderson (Alan Stewart), Sarah Marshall (Agnes Stewart), Mabel Albertson (Mrs Stewart).
SCREENPLAY Irving Ravetch, Harriet Frank Jr, from material by William Faulkner
PHOTOGRAPHY Joseph La Shelle
EDITOR Louis R. Loeffler
RUNNING TIME 117 minutes
PRODUCED BY Jerry Wald

28 The Roots of Heaven (Darryl F. ▽ Zanuck Productions)
DIRECTOR John Huston
CAST Trevor Howard (Morel), Juliette Greco (Minna), Errol Flynn (Forsythe),

Eddie Albert (Abe Fields), Orson Welles
(Cy Sedgwick), Paul Lukas (Saint-Denis),
Herbert Lom (Orsini), Gregoire Aslan
(Habib), Andre Luguet (The Governor),
Friedrich Ledebur (Peer Qvist), Edric
Connor (Waitari), Olivier Hussenot (The
Baron), Pierre Dudan (Major Scholscher),
Francis de Wolff (Father Fargue)
SCREENPLAY Romain Gary and Patrick
Leigh-Fermor, based on the former's novel
PHOTOGRAPHY Oswald Morris
EDITOR Russell Lloyd
RUNNING TIME 125 minutes
PRODUCED BY Darryl F. Zanuck

1959

29 Compulsion (Darryl F. Zanuck △
Productions)
DIRECTOR Richard Fleischer
CAST Dean Stockwell (Judd Steiner),
Bradford Dillman (Artie Straus), E. G.
Marshall (Horn), Orson Welles (Jonathan
Wilk), Diane Varsi (Ruth Evans), Martin
Milner (Sid), Richard Anderson (Max),
Robert Simon (Lt Johnson), Edward Binns
(Tom Daly)
SCREENPLAY Richard Murphy, based on the
novel by Meyer Levin
PHOTOGRAPHY William C. Mellor
EDITOR William Reynolds
RUNNING TIME 103 minutes
PRODUCED BY Richard D. Zanuck

30 Ferry to Hong Kong (A Lewis △
Gilbert Production)
DIRECTOR Lewis Gilbert
CAST Curt Jurgens (Mark Conrad), Orson
Welles (Captain Hart), Sylvia Syms (Liz
Ferrers), Jeremy Spenser (Miguel
Henriques), Noel Purcell (Joe Skinner),
Margaret Withers (Miss Carter), John
Wallace (Police Inspector), Roy Chiao
(Johnny Sing-Up), Shelley Shen (Foo Soo).
SCREENPLAY Vernon Harris, Lewis Gilbert,
based on a novel by Max Catto
PHOTOGRAPHY Otto Heller
EDITOR Peter Hunt
RUNNING TIME 113 minutes
PRODUCED BY George Maynard

31 Austerlitz (The Battle of Austerlitz) ▽
(Compagnie Francaise de Production
Internationale/Societe Cinematographique
Lyre Films [Paris]/Galatea [Rome]/Michael
Arthur Film [Vaduz]/Dubrava Film
[Zagreb])
DIRECTOR Abel Gance
CAST Pierre Mondy (Napoleon Bonaparte),
Jean Mercure (Talleyrand), Jack Palance
(General Weirother), Georges Marchal
(Lannes), Jean-Marc Bory (Soult), Orson
Welles (Fulton), Michel Simon (d'Alboise,
le Grognard), Jean-Louis Horbette
(Constant), Jacques Polycarpe Pavloff
(General Koutouzoff), Lucien Raimbourg
(Fouche), Maurice Teynac (Schulmeister),
Jean-Louis Trintignant (Segur), Martine
Carol (Josephine), Leslie Caron (Mlle de
Vaudey), Claudia Cardinale (Pauline),
Rossano Brazzi (Lucien Bonaparte), Elvire

Popesco (Laetitia), Anna Maria Ferrero
(Elise), Ettore Manni (Murat), Claude
Conty (Prince Dolgoroukow), Daniela
Rocca (Caroline), Andre Certes (Berthier),
Jean Marais (Carnot), Nelly Kaplan (Mme
Recamier), Anna Moffo (La Grassini),
Roland Bartrop (Nelson), Anthony Stuart
(Pitt), Pierre Tabard (Langeron), Randall
Whitworth (Davout d'Auerstaedt), Vittorio
De Sica (Pope Pius VII), Jean-Francois
Remy (Cadoddal), Jean-Louis Richard
(Enghien)
SCREENPLAY Abel Gance in collaboration
with Roger Richebe
PHOTOGRAPHY Henri Alekan, Robert
Juillard
EDITORS Leonide Azar, Yvonne Martin
RUNNING TIME 123 minutes
PRODUCED BY Alexandre and Michael
Salkind

32 David e Golia (David and Goliath) (ANSA)

DIRECTOR Richard Pottier, Ferdinando Baldi
CAST Orson Welles (Saul), Eleanora Rossi-Drago (Merab), Ivo Payer (David), Giulia Rubina (Michal), Massimo Serator (Abner), Pierre Cressoy (Jonathan), Edward Hilton (Prophet Samuel), Kronos (Goliath), Furio Meniconi (King Asrod), Luigi Tosi (Benjamin Di Gaba), Dante Maggio (Cret), Ugo Sasso (Huro), Umberto Fiz (Lazar), and Carlo D'Angelo, Gabriele Tinti, Ileana Danelli, Carla Foscari, Fabrizio Cappucci, Roberto Miali, Renato Terra and Emma Baron.
SCREENPLAY Umberto Scarpelli, Gino Mangini, Emimmo Salvi, Ambrogio Molteni
PHOTOGRAPHY Adalberto Albertini, Carlo Fiore

EDITOR Franco Fraticelli
RUNNING TIME 93 minutes, originally 110 minutes
PRODUCED BY Emimmo Salvi

1960

33 Crack in the Mirror (Darryl F. △ Zanuck)

DIRECTOR Richard Fleischer
CAST Juliette Greco (Eponine/Florence), Bradford Dillman (Larnier/Claude), Orson Welles (Hagolin/Lamorciere), William Lucas (Kerstner), Alexander Knox (President), Catherine Lacey (Mother Superior), Maurice Teynac (Doctor), Austin Willis (Hurtelaut), Cec Linder (Murzeau), Eugene Deckers (Magre), Yves Brainville (Prosecutor).
SCREENPLAY Mark Canfield, based on Marcel Haedrich's novel
PHOTOGRAPHY William C. Mellor
EDITOR Roger Dwyre
RUNNING TIME 97 minutes
PRODUCED BY Darryl F. Zanuck

1960

34 I Tartari (The Tartars) (Lux)

DIRECTOR Richard Thorpe
CAST Orson Welles (Burundai), Victor Mature (Oleg), Liana Orfei (Helga), Arnoldo Foa (Chu-Ling), Bella Cortez (Samja), Folco Lulli (Togrul), Luciano Marin (Eric), Furio Meniconi (Sigrun) and Pietro Ceccarelli, Renato Terra and Spartaco Nale
SCREENPLAY Sabatino Ciuffni, Ambrogio Molteni, Gaio Fratini, Oreste Palella, Emimmo Salvi, Julian De Kassel
PHOTOGRAPHY Amerigo Gengarelli
EDITOR Maurizio Lucidi
RUNNING TIME 83 minutes, originally 105 minutes
PRODUCED BY Richard Gualino

1961

35 La Fayette (Films Copernic [Paris]/ ▽ Cosmos Film [Rome])

DIRECTOR Jean Dréville
CAST Michel Le Royer (La Fayette), Jack Hawkins (Gen Cornwallis), Orson Welles (Benjamin Franklin), Howard St John (George Washington), Vittorio De Sica (Bancroft), Edmund Purdom (Silas Deane), Jacques Castelot (Duc d'Ayen), Folco Lulli (Le Boursier), Wolfgang Preiss (Baron Kalb), Liselotte Pulver (Marie Antoinette), Albert Rémy (Louis XVI), Georges Rivière (Vergennes), Renée Saint-Cyr (Duchesse d'Ayen), Rosanna Schiaffino (Comtesse de

Simiane), Pascale Audret (Mme de La Fayette), Gilles Brissac (Monsieur), Henri Amilien (Ségur), Roger Bontemps (La Bergerie), Jean-Roger Caussimon (Maurepas), Sylvie Coste (Aglae), Christian Melsen (Gen Philip), Claude Naudes (Abbé de Cour), Roland Rodier (Mauroy), Rene Rozen (Lauzun), Lois Bolton, Jean Degrave, Jean-Jacques Delbo, Michel Galabru, Jean Lanier, Antony Stuart and Henri Tisot
SCREENPLAY Jean-Bernard Luc, Suzanne Arduini, Jacques Sigurd, Francois Ponthier, Jean Dréville, Maurice Jacquin
PHOTOGRAPHY Claude Renoir, Robert Hubert
EDITOR René Le Hanaff
RUNNING TIME 112 minutes, originally 158 minutes
PRODUCED BY Maurice Jacquin

1962

36 The Trial (French title: **Le Procès**) △
(Paris Europa Productions [Paris]/FI–C–IT [Rome]/Hisa-Films [Munich])
DIRECTOR Orson Welles
CAST Anthony Perkins (Joseph K.), Orson Welles (Hastler), Jeanne Moreau (Miss Burstner), Romy Schneider (Leni), Elsa Martinelli (Hilda), Suzanne Flon (Miss Pittl), Madeleine Robinson (Mrs Grubach), Akim Tamiroff (Block), Arnoldo Foa (Inspector), Fernand Ledoux (Clerk of the Court), Maurice Teynac (Director of K's

office), Billie Kearns (1st Police Officer), Jess Hahn (2nd Police Officer), William Chappell (Titorelli), Raoul Delfosse, Karl Studer and Jean-Claude Remoleux (Executioners), Wolfgang Reichmann (Usher), Thoms Holtzmann (Student), Maydra Shore (Irmie), Max Haufler (Uncle Max), Michel Lonsdale (Priest), Max Buchsbaum (Judge), Van Doude (Archivist in cut scenes), Katina Paxinou (Scientist in cut scenes).
SCREENPLAY Orson Welles, based on the novel *Der Prozess* by Franz Kafka
PHOTOGRAPHY Edmond Richard
EDITORS Yvonne Martin, Denise Baby, Fritz Mueller
RUNNING TIME 120 minutes, English version, 118 minutes
PRODUCED BY Alexander and Michael Salkind

37 RoGoPaG (Arco Film/Cineriz/Lyre Film)
Illibatezza (Virginity)
DIRECTOR/SCREENPLAY Roberto Rossellini
CAST Rosanna Schiaffino, Bruce Balaban, Maria Pia Schiaffino
PHOTOGRAPHY Luciano Trasatti
Il Nuovo Mondo (The New World)
DIRECTOR/SCREENPLAY Jean-Luc Godard
CAST Jean-Marc Bory, Alexandra Stewart
PHOTOGRAPHY Jean Rabier
La Ricotta (Cream Cheese)
DIRECTOR/SCREENPLAY Pier Paolo Pasolini
CAST Orson Welles (The Director), Mario

Cipriani
PHOTOGRAPHY Tonino Delli Colli
Il Pollo Ruspante (The Free Range Chicken)
DIRECTOR/SCREENPLAY Ugo Gregoretti
CAST Ugo Tognazzi, Lisa Gastoni
PHOTOGRAPHY Mario Bernardo
PRODUCED BY Alfredo Bini

1963

38 The V.I.P.s (MGM) △
DIRECTOR Anthony Asquith
CAST Elizabeth Taylor (Frances Andros), Richard Burton (Paul Andros), Louis Jourdan (Marc Champselle), Elsa Martinelli (Gloria Gritti), Margaret Rutherford (Duchess of Brighton), Maggie Smith (Miss Mead), Rod Taylor (Les Mangrum), Orson Welles (Max Buda), Linda Christian (Miriam Marshall), Dennis Price (Commander Millbank), Richard Wattis (Sanders), Ronald Fraser (Joslin), David Frost (Reporter), Robert Coote (John Coburn), Joan Benham (Miss Potter), Michael Hordern (Airport Director), Lance Percival (BOAC Official), Martin Miller (Dr Schwutzbacher), Peter Sallis (Doctor), Stringer Davis (Hotel Waiter), Clifton Jones (Jamaican Passenger), Moyra Fraser (Air Hostess).
SCREENPLAY Terence Rattigan
PHOTOGRAPHY Jack Hildyard
EDITOR Frank Clarke
RUNNING TIME 119 minutes
PRODUCED BY Anatole de Grunwald

"MARCO, THE MAGNIFICENT"

1964

**39 La Fabuleuse Aventure de Marco △
Polo** (The Fabulous Adventures of Marco
Polo) (US title: **Marco the Magnificent!**)
(Ittac/SNC [Paris]/Prodi Cinematografica
[Rome]/Avala Film [Belgrade]/Mounir
Rafla [Cairo]/Italaf Kaboul [Kabul])
DIRECTOR Denys de la Patelliere, Noel
Howard
CAST Horst Buchholz (Marco Polo),
Anthony Quinn (Kublai Khan), Akim
Tamiroff (Old Man of the Mountain),
Robert Hossein (Prince Nayam), Omar
Sharif (Sheik Alaou), Elsa Martinelli (Lady

with the Whip), Orson Welles
(Ackermann), Gregoire Aslan (Achmed
Abudullah), Massimo Girotti (Nicolo
Polo), Folco Lulli (Spinello), Lee Sue Moon
(Chinese Princess), Mansoureh Rihai
(Taha), Bruno Cremer (1st Templar),
Jacques Monod (2nd Templar), Guido
Alberti (Pope Gregory X), Mica Orlovic
(Matteo Polo), Virginia Onorato.
SCREENPLAY Raoul Levy, Denys de la
Patelliere
PHOTOGRAPHY Armand Thirard
EDITORS Jacqueline Thiedot, Noelle Balenci
RUNNING TIME 115 minutes
PRODUCED BY Raoul Levy

1965

▽ **40 Paris Brule-t-Il? (Is Paris Burning?)**
(Transcontinental/Marianne)
DIRECTOR René Clement
CAST Gert Fröbe (General Dietrich von
Choltitz), Orson Welles (Consul Raoul
Nordling), Bruno Crémer (Colonel Rol),
Alain Delon (Jacques Chaban-Delmas),
Pierre Vaneck (Major Roger Gallois),
Claude Rich (General Jacques Leclerc),
Jean-Pierre Cassel (Lt Henri Karcher),
Jean-Paul Belmondo (Morandat), Leslie
Caron (Françoise Labe), Marie Versini
(Claire), Wolfgang Preiss (Ebernach), Kirk
Douglas (General George Patton), Glenn
Ford (General Omar Bradley), Claude
Dauphin (Lebel), Pierre Dux (Alexander
Parodi), Daniel Gélin (Yves Bayet), Michel
Piccoli (Edgard Pisani), Charles Boyer
(Charles Monod), Anthony Perkins (GI),
Jean-Louis Trintigant (Serge), Sacha Pitoeff
(Joliot-Curie), Simone Signoret (Café
Proprietress), Robert Stack (General Edwin
Sibert), Yves Montand (Marcel Bizien),
George Chakiris (GI), Harry Meyen (Von
Arnim), Billy Frick (Adolf Hitler), Skip
Ward (GI), Michel Etcheverry (Luizet),
Toni Taffin (Labe), Bernard Fresson
(Liaison Agent), Michel Gonzales
(Jacques), Christian Rode, Georges Géret,
Michel Berger, Hannes Messemer, Albert
Rémy, Karl Otto Alberty, Roger Lumont.
SCREENPLAY Gore Vidal, Francis Ford
Coppola, based on the book by Larry
Collins and Dominique Lapierre
PHOTOGRAPHY Marcel Grignon
EDITOR Robert Lawrence
RUNNING TIME 165 minutes (English
version)
PRODUCED BY Paul Graetz

1966

41 Chimes at Midnight (US title: △
Falstaff, Spanish title: **Campanadas a
Medianoches**) (Internacional Films
Espanola [Madrid]/Alpine [Basle])

DIRECTOR Orson Welles
CAST Orson Welles (Sir John Falstaff),
Keith Baxter (Prince Hal, later King Henry
V), John Gielgud (King Henry IV), Jeanne
Moreau (Doll Tearsheet), Margaret
Rutherford (Mistress Quickly), Norman
Rodway (Henry Percy, called Hotspur),
Marina Vlady (Kate Percy), Alan Webb
(Justice Shallow), Walter Chiari (Silence),
Michael Aldridge (Pistol), Tony Beckley
(Poins), Fernando Rey (Worcester),
Andrew Faulds (Westmoreland), Jose Nieto
(Northumberland), Jeremy Rowe (Prince
John), Beatrice Welles (Falstaff's Page),
Paddy Bedford (Bardolph), Julio Pena,
Fernando Hilbert, Andres Mejuto, Keith
Pyott, Charles Farrell.
EXECUTIVE PRODUCER Alessandro Tasca
SCREENPLAY Orson Welles, adapted from
the plays *Richard II*, *Henry IV Parts I and
II*, *Henry V* and *The Merry Wives of
Windsor* by William Shakespeare and (for
the commentary) *The Chronicles of England*
by Raphael Holinshed
PHOTOGRAPHY Edmond Richard
EDITOR Fritz Mueller
RUNNING TIME 119 minutes, 115 minutes in
Great Britain
PRODUCED BY Emiliano Piedra, Angel
Escolano

42 A Man for All Seasons (Highland) ▽
DIRECTOR Fred Zinnemann
CAST Paul Scofield (Sir Thomas More),
Robert Shaw (Henry VIII), Wendy Hiller
(Alice More), Leo McKern (Thomas
Cromwell), Orson Welles (Cardinal
Wolsey), Susannah York (Margaret), Nigel
Davenport (Duke of Norfolk), John Hurt
(Richard Rich), Corin Redgrave (William
Roper), Colin Blakely (Matthew), Cyril
Luckham (Archbishop Cranmer), Jack
Gwillim (Chief Justice), Thomas Heathcote
(Boatman), Yootha Joyce (Averil Machin),
Anthony Nicholls (King's Representative),
John Nettleton (Jailer), Eira Heath
(Matthew's Wife), Molly Urquhart (Maid),
Paul Hardwick (Courtier), Michael Latimer
(Norfolk's Aide), Philip Brack (Captain of
Guard), Martin Boddey (Governor of
Tower), Eric Mason (Executioner), Matt
Zimmerman (Messenger), Vanessa
Redgrave (Anne Boleyn)
EXECUTIVE PRODUCER William N. Graf
SCREENPLAY Robert Bolt, based on his own
play
PHOTOGRAPHY Ted Moore
EDITOR Ralph Kemplen
RUNNING TIME 120 minutes
PRODUCED BY Fred Zinnemann

43 The Sailor from Gibraltar (Woodfall)
DIRECTOR Tony Richardson
CAST Jeanne Moreau (Anna), Ian Bannen (Alan), Vanessa Redgrave (Sheila), Orson Welles (Louis from Mozambique), Zia Mohyeddin (Noori), Hugh Griffith (Llewellyn), Umberto Orsini (Postcard Vendor), Erminio Spalla (Eolo), Eleanor Brown (Carla), Gabriella Pallotta (Girl at Dance), Arnoldo Foa (Man on Train), Claudio De Renzi (Jeannot), Fausto Tozzi (Captain), John Hurt (John), Theodor Roubanis (Theo), Massimo Sarchielli (Massimo), Guglielmo Spoletini (Guglielmo), Wolfgang Hillinger (Wolf), Brad Moore (Brad).
SCREENPLAY Christopher Isherwood, Don Magner, Tony Richardson, based on the novel *Le Marin de Gibraltar* by Marguerite Duras
PHOTOGRAPHY Raoul Coutard
EDITOR William Blunden
RUNNING TIME 91 minutes
PRODUCED BY Oscar Lewenstein, Neil Hartley

1967

44 Casino Royale (Famous Artists)
DIRECTORS John Huston, Ken Hughes, Val Guest, Robert Parrish, Joe McGrath
CAST David Niven (Sir James Bond), Peter Sellers (Evelyn Tremble), Ursula Andress (Vesper Lynd), Orson Welles (Le Chiffre), Joanna Pettet (Mata Bond), Daliah Lavi (The Detainer), Deborah Kerr (Agent Mimi), Woody Allen (Jimmy Bond), William Holden (Ransome), Charles Boyer (Le Grand), John Huston ('M'), Kurt Kasnar (Smernov), Terence Cooper (Cooper), Barbara Bouchet (Moneypenny), Angela Scoular (Buttercup), Tracey Crisp (Heather), Elaine Taylor (Peg), Gabriella Licudi (Eliza), Jacky Bisset (Miss Goodthighs), Alexandra Bastedo (Meg), Anna Quayle (Frau Hoffner), Derek Nimmo (Hadley), George Raft (Himself), Jean-Paul Belmondo (French Legionnaire), Peter O'Toole (Piper), Stirling Moss (Driver), Ronnie Corbett (Polo), Colin Gordon (Casino Director), Bernard Cribbins (Taxi Driver), Tracy Reed (Fang Leader), John Bluthal (Casino Doorman/MI5 Man), Geoffrey Bayldon ('Q'), John Wells ('Q''s Assistant), Duncan Macrae (Inspector Mathis), Graham Stark (Cashier), Chic Murray (Chic), Jonathan Routh (John), Richard Wattis (British Army Officer), Vladek Sheybal (Le Chiffre's Representative), Percy Herbert (1st Piper),

Penny Riley (Control Girl), Jeanne Roland (Captain of Guards)
SCREENPLAY Wolf Mankowitz, John Law, Michael Sayers, suggested by the novel by Ian Fleming
PHOTOGRAPHY Jack Hildyard
EDITOR Bill Lenny
RUNNING TIME 131 minutes
PRODUCED BY Charles K. Feldman, Jerry Bresler

45 I'll Never Forget What's'is Name △
(Scimitar, A Universal Presentation)
DIRECTOR Michael Winner
CAST Orson Welles (Jonathan Lute), Oliver Reed (Andrew Quint), Carol White (Georgina), Harry Andrews (Gerald Sater), Michael Hordern (Headmaster), Wendy Craig (Louise Quint), Marianne Faithfull (Josie), Norman Rodway (Nicholas), Frank Finlay (Chaplain), Harvey Hall (Maccabee), Ann Lynn (Carla), Lyn Ashley (Susannah), Veronica Clifford (Anna), Edward Fox (Walter), Stuart Cooper (Lewis Force), Roland Curram (Eldrich), Peter Graves (Bankman), Mark Burns (Michael Cornwall), Mark Eden (Kellaway), Josephine Rueg (Marian), Mona Chong (Vietnamese Girl), Robert Mill (Galloway), Terence Seward (Pinchin)
SCREENPLAY Peter Draper
PHOTOGRAPHY Otto Heller
EDITOR Bernard Gribble
RUNNING TIME 97 minutes
PRODUCED BY Michael Winner

46 Oedipus the King (Crossroads/ ▷
Universal)
DIRECTOR Philip Saville
CAST Christopher Plummer (Oedipus), Lilli Palmer (Jocasta), Richard Johnson (Creon), Orson Welles (Tiresias), Cyril

Cusack (Messenger), Roger Livesey (Shepherd), Donald Sutherland (Chorus Leader), Alexis Mantheakis (Palace Official), Demos Starenios (Priest), Friedrich Ledebur (King Laius), Oenone Luke (Antigone), Cressida Luke (Ismene), Costas Themos, Paul Roche, Minos Argyrakis, Takis Emmanouel, George Dialegmenos (Members of the Chorus), Mary Xenoudaki, Jenny Daminanopoulou,

Diana J. Reed (Jocasta's Handmaidens).
SCREENPLAY Michael Luke, Philip Saville, based on the play by Sophocles, translated by Paul Roche
PHOTOGRAPHY Walter Lassally
EDITOR Paul Davies
RUNNING TIME 97 minutes
PRODUCED BY Michael Luke

1968

47 The Immortal Story (French title: **Histoire Immortelle**) (ORTF/Albina Films)
DIRECTOR Orson Welles
CAST Orson Welles (Mr Clay), Jeanne Moreau (Virginie Ducrot), Roger Coggio (Elishama Levinsky), Norman Eshley (Paul), Fernando Rey (Merchant)
SCREENPLAY Orson Welles, based on the novella by Isak Dinesen (Karen Blixen)
PHOTOGRAPHY Willy Kurant
EDITORS Yolande Maurette, Marcelle Pluet, Francoise Garnault, Claude Farny
RUNNING TIME 60 minutes
PRODUCED BY Micheline Rozan

48 House of Cards (Westward)
DIRECTOR John Guillermin
CAST George Peppard (Reno Davis), Inger Stevens (Anne de Villemont), Keith Michell (Hubert Morillon), Orson Welles (Charles Leschenhaut), William Job (Bernard Bourdon), Maxine Audley (Matilde Vosiers), Peter Bayliss (Edmond Vosiers), Patience Collier (Gabrielle de Villemont), Barnaby Shaw (Paul de Villemont), Rosemary Dexter (Daniella Braggi), Perrette Pradier (Jeanne Marie), Ralph Michael (Claude de Gonde), Raoul Delfosse (Louis LeBuc), Genevieve Cluny (Veronique), Ave Ninchi (Signora Braggi), Renzo Palmer (The Monk), Francesco Mule (Trevi Policeman), Jacques Stany (Georges), Paule Albert (Sophie), James Mishler (Hardee), Jean Louis (Driot), Jacques Rous (Maguy).
SCREENPLAY James P. Bonner
PHOTOGRAPHY Piero Portalupi
EDITOR J. Terry Williams
RUNNING TIME 105 minutes
PRODUCED BY Dick Berg

49 Kampf um Rom (Fight for Rome, *AKA* **The Last Roman**) (CCC [West Berlin] production in conjunction with Studioul Cinematografic [Bucharest])
DIRECTOR Robert Siodmak
CAST Laurence Harvey (Cethegus), Orson Welles (Justinian), Sylva Koscina (Theodora), Honor Blackman (Amalaswintha), Robert Hoffmann (Totila), Harriet Andersson (Mathaswintha), Michael Dunn (Narses), Ingrid Brett (Julia), Lang Jeffries (Belisar).
SCREENPLAY Ladislas Fodor
PHOTOGRAPHY Richard Angst
EDITOR Alfred Srp
RUNNING TIME Part I: 103 minutes.
　　　　　　Part II: 84 minutes.
　　　　　　condensed version (1973):
　　　　　　94 minutes
PRODUCED BY Artur Brauner

50 The Southern Star (French title: ▽
L'etoile du Sud) (Euro France Films/
Capitole Films [Paris]/Columbia British
[London])
DIRECTOR Sidney Hayers
CAST George Segal (Dan Rockland), Ursula
Andress (Erica Kramer), Orson Welles
(Plankett), Ian Hendry (Karl Ludwig),
Michel Constantin (Jose), Harry Andrews
(Kramer), Johnny Sekka (Matakit),
Georges Geret (Andre), Sylvain (Louis),
Guy Delorme (Michel), Van Dooren (Man
in Bar), and the National Ballet of Senegal.
SCREENPLAY David Purcell, John Seddon,
based on the novel by Jules Verne
PHOTOGRAPHY Raoul Coutard
EDITOR Tristam Cones
RUNNING TIME 105 minutes (English version)
PRODUCED BY Roger Duchet

51 Tepepa (Filmamerica, SIAP, Roma
PEFSA, Madrid))
DIRECTOR Giulio Petroni
CAST Tomas Milian, Orson Welles (Colonel
Cascarro), John Steiner, Jose Torres, Ana
Mari Lanciaprima, Paloma Cela, Rafael
Hernandez, Luciano Casamonica.
SCREENPLAY Franco Solinas, Ivan Della
Mea
PHOTOGRAPHY Francisco Marin
RUNNING TIME 105 minutes

1969

52 Start the Revolution without me (Norbud
Films)
DIRECTOR Bud Yorkin

CAST Gene Wilder (Claude Coupe/Phillipe
Di Sisi), Donald Sutherland (Charles
Coupe/Pierre Di Sisi), Hugh Griffith (Louis
XVI), Jack MacGowran (Jacques
Cabriolet), Billie Whitelaw (Marie
Antoinette), Victor Spinetti (Duke
d'Escargot), Ewa Aulin (Princess
Christina), Helen Fraser (Mimi Montage),
Rosalind Knight (Helene Di Sisi), Maxwell
Shaw (Comte Di Sisi), George A. Cooper
(Doctor), Graham Stark (Coupe Father),
Harry Fowler (Jacques' Lieutenant),
Murray Melvin (Blind Man), Ken Parry
(Doctor Boileau), Jacques Maury (Lt
Sorel), Denise Coffey (Anne Duval)
EXECUTIVE PRODUCER Norman Lear
SCREENPLAY Fred Freeman, Lawrence, J.
Cohen
PHOTOGRAPHY Jean Tournier
EDITOR Ferris Webster
RUNNING TIME 90 minutes
PRODUCED BY Bud Yorkin

53 Bitka na Neretvi (UK video release title:
The Battle of the River Neretva)
(Dobrovoljacka [Sarajevo]/Eickberg
[Monaco]/Igor Film [Rome])
DIRECTOR Veljko Bulajic
CAST Yul Brynner (Vlado), Orson Welles
(Senator), Curt Jurgens (General Lohring),
Sergei Bondarchuk (Martin), Oleg Vidov
(Nikola), Milena Dravic (Nada), Franco
Nero (Captain Riva), Sylva Koscina
(Danitsa), Hardy Kruger (Colonel
Karntzer), Ljubisa Samardjic (Novak),
Lojze Rozman (Ivan), Boris Dvornik

(Stipe), Anthony Dawson (General
Morelli), Howard Ross (Seargeant Mario),
Charles Millot (Djubka), Bata Zivojinovic
(Stole), Fabijan Sovagovic (Mad Bosco),
Pavlo Viusic (Jordan), Robert Hoffmann.
SCREENPLAY Ugo Pirro, Patko Djurovic,
Veljko Bulajic, Stevo Bulajic (US version:
Alfred Hayes)
PHOTOGRAPHY Tomislav Pinter
EDITOR Vanja Bjenjas
RUNNING TIME 175 minutes (UK video
release running time: 127 minutes)
PRODUCED BY Steve Previn

54 Mihai Viteasul (**Michael the Brave** *AKA*
The Last Crusade) (Romania Film
[Bucuresti])
DIRECTOR Sergiu Nicolaescu
CAST Amza Pellea, Irina Gardescu, Florin
Persic, Septimiu Sever, Ilarion Ciobau,
Sergiu Nicolaescu, Mircea Albulescu, Ioana
Bulca, Gh Kovacs, Olga Tudorache, Aurel
Rogalski, Ion Besciu, Alexandru Herescu,
Colea Rautu, Orson Welles' appearance
uncredited.
SCREENPLAY Titus Popovici
PHOTOGRAPHY George Cornea
EDITOR Ioland Mintuleascu
RUNNING TIME 120 minutes

55 The Kremlin Letter (20th Century ▷
Fox)
DIRECTOR John Huston
CAST Richard Boone (Ward), Bibi
Andersson (Erika Boeck), Max von Sydow

(Colonel Vladimir Kosnov), Patrick O'Neal (Lt Commander Charles Rone), Orson Welles (Aleksei Bresnavitch), Ronald Radd (Potkin), Nigel Green (Janis, alias 'The Whore'), Dean Jagger ('The Highwayman', Lila Kedrova (Madame Sophie), Barbara Parkins (B. A.), George Sanders ('The Warlock'), Raf Vallone ('The Puppet Maker'), Micheal MacLiammoir ('Sweet Alice'), Sandor Eles (Grodin), Niall MacGinnis (Erector Set), Anthony Chinn (Kitai), Guy Deghy (Professor), John Huston (Admiral), Fulvia Ketoff (Sonia), Vonetta McGee (Negress), Marc Lawrence (Priest), Cyril Shaps (Police Doctor), Christopher Sanford (Rudolph), Hana-Maria Pravda (Mrs Kazar), George Pravda (Kazar), Ludmilla Dudarova (Mrs Potkin), Dimitri Tamarov (Ilya), Pehr-Olof Siren (Receptionist), Daniel Smid (Waiter), Victor Beaumont (Dentist), Steve Zacharias (Dittomachine), Laura Forin (Elena), Saara Rannin (Mikhail's Mother), Rune Sandlunds (Mikhail), Sacha Carafa (Mrs Grodin).
SCREENPLAY John Huston, Gladys Hill, based on the novel by Noel Behn
PHOTOGRAPHY Ted Scaife
EDITOR Russell Lloyd
RUNNING TIME 121 minutes
PRODUCED BY Carter De Haven, Sam Wiesenthal

1970

56 Una su Tredici (12 + 1) (COFCI-CEF)
DIRECTOR Nicolas Gessner
CAST Sharon Tate (Pat), Orson Welles (Markau), Vittorio Gassmann (Mike), Vittorio De Sica (Di Seta), Mylene Demongeot (Judy), Terry Thomas (Albert), Tim Brooke Taylor (Jackie).
SCREENPLAY Marc Beham, Nicolas Gessner

PHOTOGRAPHY Giuseppi Ruzzolini
RUNNING TIME 95 minutes
PRODUCED BY Claude Giroux

57 Catch–22 (Paramount) △
DIRECTOR Mike Nichols
CAST Alan Arkin (Capt Yossarian), Martin Balsam (Col Cathcart), Richard Benjamin (Major Danby), Art Garfunkel (Capt Nately), Jack Gilford (Doc Daneeka), Buck

Henry (Lt Col Korn), Bob Newhart (Major Major), Anthony Perkins (Chaplain Tappman), Paula Prentiss (Nurse Duckett), Martin Sheen (Lt Dobbs), Jon Voight (Milo Minderbinder), Orson Welles (Gen Dreedle), Seth Allen (Hungry Joe), Robert Balaban (Capt Orr), Susanne Benton (Gen Dreedle's WAC), Peter Bonerz (Capt McWatt), Norman Fell (Sgt Towser), Chuck Grodin (Aardvark), Austin Pendleton (Col Moodus), Gina Rovere

CAST Orson Welles (Michelangelo), Edith Evans (Queen Christian), Dirk Bogarde (Prince Charlie), Ralph Richardson (Guide).
SCREENPLAY Harry Rosky
PHOTOGRAPHY Aldo Tonti
EDITOR Donald J. Cohen
RUNNING TIME 90 minutes

◁ **60 A Safe Place** (BBS Productions for Columbia)
DIRECTOR Henry Jaglom
CAST Tuesday Weld (Noah [Susan]), Jack Nicholson (Mitch), Orson Welles (Magician), Philip Proctor (Fred), Gwen Welles (Bari), Dov Lawrence (Larry), Fanny Birkenmaier (Maid), Rhonda Alfaro (Little Girl in Rowboat), Sylvia Zapp (5-year-old Susan), Richard Finnochio, Barbara Flood, Roger Garrett, Jordan Hahn, Francesca Hilton, Julie Robinson, Jennifer Walker (Noah's Friends).
SCREENPLAY Henry Jaglom
PHOTOGRAPHY Dick Kratina
EDITOR Pieter Bergema
RUNNING TIME 92 minutes
PRODUCED BY Bert Schneider

1971

▽ **61 Treasure Island** (Massfilms [London]/ Les Productions F D L [Paris]/CCC Filmkunst [Berlin]/Eguiluz Films [Madrid])
DIRECTOR John Hough
CAST Orson Welles (Long John Silver), Kim Burfield (Jim Hawkins), Lionel Stander (Billy Bones), Walter Slezak (Squire Trelawney), Angel Del Pozo (Doctor Livesey), Rik Battaglia (Captain Smollett), Maria Rohm (Mrs Hawkins), Paul Muller (Blind Pew), Jean Lefevbre (Ben Gunn),

(Nately's Whore), Olympia Carlisli (Luciana), Marcel Dalio (Old Man), Eva Maltagliati (Old Woman), Liam Dunn (Father), Elizabeth Wilson (Mother), Richard Libertini (Brother), Jonathon Korkes (Snowden).
SCREENPLAY Buck Henry, based on the novel by Joseph Heller
PHOTOGRAPHY David Watkin
EDITOR Sam O'Steen
RUNNING TIME 122 minutes
PRODUCED BY John Calley, Martin Ransohoff

◁ **58 Waterloo** (Dino De Laurentiis Cinematografica [Rome]/Mosfilm [Moscow])
DIRECTOR Sergei Bondarchuk
CAST Rod Steiger (Napoleon), Christopher Plummer (Wellington), Orson Welles (Louis XVIII), Jack Hawkins (General Picton), Virginia McKenna (Duchess of Richmond), Dan O'Herlihy (Marshal Ney), Rupert Davies (Gordon), Philippe Forquet (La Bedoyere), Gianni Garko (Drouot), Ivo Garrani (Soult), Ian Ogilvy (De Lancey), Michael Wilding (Ponsonby), Sergei Zakhariadze (Blucher), Terence Alexander (Uxbridge), Andrea Checchi (Sauret), Donal Donelly (O'Connor), Charles Millot (Grouchy), Eughenj Samoilov (Cambronne), Oleg Vidov (Tomlinson), Charles Borromel (Mulholland), Peter Davies (Lord Hay), Veronica De Laurentiis (Magdalene Hall), Vladimir Durjnikov (Gerard), Willoughby Gray (Ramsey), Roger Green (Duncan), Orso Maria Guerrini (Officer), Richard Heffer (Mercer), Orazio Orlando (Constant), John Savident (Muffling), Jeffry Wickham (Colborne), Susan Wood (Sarah), Ghennady Yudin (Chactas).

SCREENPLAY H. A. L. Craig, Sergei Bondarchuk, Vittorio Bonicelli
PHOTOGRAPHY Armando Nannuzzi
EDITOR E. V. Michajlova
RUNNING TIME 132 minutes
PRODUCED BY Dino De Laurentiis

59 Upon this Rock (Marstan-Rock Corporation/Sheldon-Wilson/Stanley Abrams Production)
DIRECTOR Harry Rosky

Michael Garland (Merry), Aldo Sambrell
(Israel Hands), Alibe (Mrs Silver),
Chinchilla (Anderson).
SCREENPLAY Wolf Mankowitz, O. W. Jeeves
(Orson Welles), based on the novel by
Robert Louis Stevenson
PHOTOGRAPHY Cecilio Paniagua
EDITOR Nicholas Wentworth
RUNNING TIME 95 minutes
PRODUCED BY Harry Alan Towers

62 Malpertuis (SOFIDOC [Brussels]/Les
Productions Artistes Associes/Societe
d'Expansion du Spectacle [Paris]/Artemis
Film [West Berlin])
DIRECTOR Harry Kumel
CAST Orson Welles (Cassavius), Susan
Hampshire (Nancy/Euryale/Alice), Michel
Bouquet (Dideloo), Mathieu Carriere
(Yann), Jean-Pierre Cassel (Lampernis),
Sylvie Vartan (Bets), Daniel Pilon (Mathias
Krook), Dora Van Der Groen (Sylvie
Dideloo), Charles Janssens (Philarete),
Walter Rilla (Eisengott), Bob Storm
(Griboin), Fanny Winkler (Mother
Griboin), Ward De Ravet (Abbot
Doucedame), Jet Naessens (Eleonore), Cara
Van Wersch (Rosalie), Jenny Van
Santvoort (Elodie), Hugo Dellas (Hans),
Gella Allaert (Gerda), Johan Troch
(Beggar), Cyriel Van Gent (Fat Man)
SCREENPLAY Jean Ferry, based on the novel
by Jean Ray
PHOTOGRAPHY Gerry Fisher
EDITOR Richard Marden
RUNNING TIME 96 minutes (originally 124
minutes), English version
PRODUCED BY Pierre Levie, Paul Laffargue

1972

◁ **63 La Décade Prodigieuse (Ten Days'
Wonder)** (Films La Boetie)
DIRECTOR Claude Chabrol
CAST Orson Welles (Theo Van Horn),
Marlene Jobert (Helene), Anthony Perkins
(Charles Van Horn), Michel Piccoli (Paul
Regis), Guido Alberti (Ludovic), Sylvana
Blasi (Woman), Giovanni Sciuto (Money
Lender), Ermmano Casanova (Old Man
With Eye Patch), Tsilla Chelton (Charles'
Mother), Eric Frisdal (Charles as a Boy),
Aline Montovani (Helene as a Girl),
Vittorio Sanipoli (Police Inspector),
Mathilde Ceccarelli, Corinne
Koeningswarter, Fabienne Gauglof.
SCREENPLAY Paul Gegauff, Paul Gardner,
Eugene Archer, based on a novel by Ellery
Queen
PHOTOGRAPHY Jean Rabier
EDITOR Jacques Gaillard
RUNNING TIME 108 minutes
PRODUCED BY Andre Genovese

◁ **64 Get to Know your Rabbit** (Warner
Brothers)
DIRECTOR Brian De Palma
CAST Tom Smothers, John Astin, Suzanne
Zenor, Samantha Jones, Allen Garfield,
Katharine Ross, Orson Welles, Hope
Summers
EXECUTIVE PRODUCER Peter Nelson
SCREENPLAY Jordan Crittenden
PHOTOGRAPHY John Alonzo
EDITORS Frank Urioste, Peter Colbert
RUNNING TIME 93 minutes
PRODUCED BY Steven Bernhardt, Paul Gaer

65 Necromancy (Zenith International △
Pictures)
DIRECTOR Bert I. Gordon
CAST Orson Welles (Mr Cato), Pamela
Franklin (Lori), Lee Purcell (Priscilla),
Michael Ontkean (Frank), Harvey Jason
(Jay), Lisa James (Georgette), Sue Bernard
(Nancy), Terry Quinn (Cato's son).
SCREENPLAY Bert I. Gordon
PHOTOGRAPHY Winton Hoch
EDITORS John Woelz
RUNNING TIME 82 minutes
PRODUCED BY Bert I. Gordon

1973

66 F For Fake (Verités et Mensonges) (Les
Films de l'Astrophore [Paris]/Saci [Tehran]/
Janus Film [Munich])
DIRECTOR Orson Welles
CAST Orson Welles, Oja Kodar, Elmyr de
Hory, Clifford Irving, Edith Irving,
Francois Reichenbach, Joseph Cotten,
Laurence Harvey, Richard Wilson, Paul
Stewart, Howard Hughes, Sasa Devcic,
Gary Graver, Andres Vincent Gomez, Julio
Palinkas, Christian Odasso, Francoise
Widoff, (offscreen) Peter Bogdanovich and
William Alland.
SCREENPLAY Orson Welles, Oja Palinkas
PHOTOGRAPHY [USA & Toussaint] Gary
Graver, [France & Ibiza] Christain Odasso
EDITORS Marie Sophie Dubus, Dominique
Engerer
RUNNING TIME 85 minutes
PRODUCED BY Dominique Antoine,
Francois Reichenbach

1976

67 The Late Great Planet Earth (Robert
Amram Films/RCR Productions in
association with the Petersen Company)
DIRECTOR Robert Amram
CAST Beaumont Bruestle (False Prophet),
Timothy Nicely (Leader of the Chase), Del
Russell (Jeremiah), Howard Whalen (John
the Apostle), Judith Roberts (The Whore of
Babylon), Frank Ferrer, Sam Gilman
Richard Hale, Robert Hackman, Abbe
Kanter.
EXECUTIVE PRODUCER Michael F. Leone
SCREENPLAY Robert Amram (Biblical
sequences), Rolf Forsberg, based on the
book by Hal Lindsey, C. C. Carlson
PHOTOGRAPHY Michael Werk
EDITORS Victor Costello, Anne Goursaud
Epstein
NARRATORS Orson Welles, Hal Lindsey
WRITTEN Orson Welles, Hal Lindsey,
Aurelio Peccei, George Wald, Norman
Borlaug, Emile Benoit, Desmond Morris,
John Gribbin, Paul Ehrlich, William
Paddock, Joseph Waggoner Jnr,
G. Kistiakowski, George Rathgens, Chaim
Herzog, Jacques Piccard, Mahesh Yogi
Maharji Ji, the Rev Moon, Robert Nisbet,
Peter Hamilton, Elm Zumwalt
RUNNING TIME 86 minutes
PRODUCED BY Robert Amram, Alan Belkin

173

Counter-Intelligence), Victor Spinetti (Dr Erich Strauss), Janet Suzman (Leni Strauss), Frederick Jaeger (Werner Mannheim), Guenter Meisner (Robert Hoffmann, Abwehr Agent in Cuba), Bernard Hepton (Milton Goldsmith, Jewish Agency Representative in Cuba), David Daker (Paul Ostermeyer, 1st Officer), Keith Barron (Mueller, Purser), David De Keyser (Joseph Joseph, Lawyer and Head of the Passengers' Committee), Ian Cullen (Steinman, Chief Radio Officer), Constantin De Goguel (Heinrich, Navigation Officer), Don Henderson (Kolmer, Engineering Officer), Brian Gilbert (Laurenz Schulman), Carl Duering (Dr von Kaempe, German Ambassador in Cuba), Anthony Higgins (Heinz Berg), Della McDermott (Julia Strauss), Genevieve West (Sarah Strauss), Milo Sperber (Rabbi), Ina Skriver (Singer), Marika Rivera (Bordello Madam), Philip Stone (Belgian Under-Secretary), Laura Gemser (Estedes' Girlfriend), Robin Halstead (SS Photographer), Bernard Kaye (Harbour Pilot), Garry McDermott (Koster, Helmsman).
SCREENPLAY Steve Shagan, David Butler, based on the book by Gordon Thomas, Max Morgan-Witts
PHOTOGRAPHY Billy Williams
EDITOR Tom Priestley
RUNNING TIME 137 minutes (originally 155 minutes)
PRODUCED BY Robert Fryer

1979

69 The Muppet Movie ITC
DIRECTOR James Frawley
CAST Charles Durning (Doc Hopper), Austin Pendleton (Max), Scott Walker ('Snake' Walker the Frog-killer), Lawrence Gabriel Jr (Sailor), Ira F. Grubman (Bartender), H. B. Haggerty (Lumberjack), Bruce Kirby (Gate Guard), Tommy Madden (One-eyed Midget), James Frawley (Waiter), Arnold Roberts (Cowboy), Edgar Bergen (Himself), Milton Berle ('Mad Man' Mooney), Mel Brooks (Professor Max Krassman), James Coburn (Owner of El Sleezo Café), Dom DeLuise (Bernie the Hollywood Agent), Elliott Gould (Beauty Contest Compere), Bob Hope (Ice Cream Vendor), Madeline Kahn (El Sleezo Patron), Carol Kane ('Myth'), Cloris Leachman (Lord's Secretary), Steve Martin (Insolent Waiter), Richard Pryor (Balloon Vendor), Telly Savalas (El Sleezo Tough), Orson Welles (Lew Lord), Paul Williams (El Sleezo Pianist)
EXECUTIVE PRODUCER Martin Starger
SCREENPLAY Jerry Juhl, Jack Burns
PHOTOGRAPHY Isidore Mankofsky
EDITOR Chris Greenbury
RUNNING TIME 97 minutes
PRODUCED BY Jim Henson

1980

70 Tajna Nikole Tesle (The Secret of Nikole Tesle) Zagreb Film-Kinematografi
DIRECTOR Krsto Papic
CAST Peter Bozovic, Orson Welles (J. P. Morgan), Strother Martin (George Westinghouse), Dennis Patrick (Thomas Edison), Oja Kodar, Boris Buzancic, Charles Millot, Ana Kavic
SCREENPLAY Ivo Bresan, Ivan Kusan
PHOTOGRAPHY Ivica Rajkovic
RUNNING TIME 120 minutes

1981

71 Butterfly Par Par Productions ▽
DIRECTOR Matt Cimber

1977

68 Voyage of the Damned (ITC △ Entertainment/Associated General Films)
DIRECTOR Stuart Rosenberg
CAST Faye Dunaway (Denise Kreisler), Max Von Sydow (Captain Gustav Schroeder), Oskar Werner (Dr Egon Kreisler), Malcolm McDowell (Max Gunther), James Mason (Dr Juan Remos, Cuban Minister of State), Orson Welles (Jose Estedes, Cuban Industrialist), Katharine Ross (Mira Hauser), Ben Gazzara (Morris Troper, European Head of Jewish Agency), Lee Grant (Lili Rosen), Sam Wanamaker (Carl Rosen), Lynne Frederick (Anna Rosen), Julie Harris (Alice Feinchild), Helmut Griem (Otto Schiendick, 2nd Class Steward), Luther Adler (Professor Weiler), Wendy Hiller (Rebecca Weiler), Nehemiah Persoff (Mr Hauser), Maria Schell (Mrs Miriam Hauser), Paul Koslo (Aaron Pozner), Jonathan Pryce (Joseph Manasse), Fernando Rey (President Bru of Cuba), Donald Houston (Dr Hans Glauner, Ship's Doctor), Michael Constantine (Luis Clasing, Hamburg-Amerika Line Agent), Jose Ferrer (Manuel Benitez, Cuban Director of Immigration), Denholm Elliott (Admiral Canaris, Head of German

CAST Stacy Keach (Jess Tyler), Pia Zadora (Kady), Orson Welles (Judge Rauch), Lois Nettleton (Belle Morgan), Edward Albert (Wash Gillespie), Stuart Whitman (Reverend Rivers), Ed McMahon (Mr Gillespie), June Lockhart (Mrs Gillespie), James Franciscus (Moke Blue), Paul Hampton (Norton), Buck Flower (Ed Lamey), Ann Dane (Jane), Greg Gault (Bridger), John O'Connor White (Billy Roy), Peter Jason (Allen), Kim Ptak (Deputy), Leigh Christian (Saleslady), Dr Abraham Rudnick (Court Stenographer), John Goff (Truck Driver), Dylan Urquidi (Danny)
EXECUTIVE PRODUCER Tino Barzie
SCREENPLAY John Goff, Matt Cimber, based on the novel *The Butterfly* by James Cain
PHOTOGRAPHY Eddy Van Der Enden
EDITORS B. A. Schoenfeld, Stan Siegel
RUNNING TIME 108 minutes
PRODUCED BY Matt Cimber

1983

72 Where is Parsifal? Slederline
DIRECTOR Henri Helman
CAST Tony Curtis (Parsifal Katzanella-Boden), Cassandra Domenica (Elba Katzanella-Boden), Erik Estrada (Henry Board II), Peter Lawford (Montague Chippendale), Ron Moody (Baron Gaspard Beersbohm), Donald Pleasence (Mackintosh), Orson Welles (Klingsor), Christopher Chaplin (Ivan), Nancy Roberts (Ruth), Vladek Sheybal (Morjack), Ava Lazar (Sheila), Jay Benedict (Luke), Edward Burnham (Trofimov), Anthony Dawson (Ripple), Victoria Burgoyne (Gabriela Veronica), Stuart Latham (Rutovitz), Simon Cloquet (Flocon), David Baxt (PR Man), Peter Poll (First Bodyguard), Sally Cranfield (Journalist), Christina Artemis (Grace), Pamela Trigg (PR Assistant), Arthur Beatty
EXECUTIVE PRODUCER Terence Young
SCREENPLAY Berta Dominguez D
PHOTOGRAPHY Norman Langley
EDITORS Russ Lloyd, Peter Hollywood
RUNNING TIME 87 minutes
PRODUCED BY Daniel Carrillo

EARLY AND UNFINISHED FILMS

1934 Too Much Johnson

1942/43 Its All True

1958/59 Don Quixote

1967/69 The Deep, aka Dead Calm, aka Dead Reckoning

1970/75 The Other Side of the Wind

1979 Never Trust an Honest Thief

1985 Is It You?

Acknowledgements

The following illustrations appear by the kind permission of:

John Russell Taylor (Frontispiece); The Billy Rose Theatre Collection, the NY Public Library: 12, 22 (B), 23, 24 (B, T), 26, 33 (T), 34, 64, 144; Popperfoto: 13, 33 (B), 36/37, 38 (B); UPI/ Bettmann: 18, 19, 35; The Photo Source: 76 (B), 111, 131 (B); Phototeque: 132 (T), 158 (TR), 162 (B); Mander & Mitchenson: 112; John Timbers: 126, 127, 128; Museum of Modern Art/Film Stills: 29 (T), 53 (TL), 73 (T), 76 (T), 147 (B); Stiftung Deutsche Kinemathek: 113 (B), 144, 149 (B), 160 (B); Library of Congress Federal Theatre Project Collection at George Mason University Library, Fairfax, Virginia: 22, 24 (T), 27.

The following illustrations appear courtesy of:

The National Film Archive: 7, 10, 14 (B), 30, 45 (T), 51 (T), 54, 56, 57, 61 (C, B), 64, 78 (L), 80 (L, T), 81, 82, 90 (C, B, R), 91, 95 (TR), 98, 100 (T), 101, 102 (C, B), 104 (B), 120 (L, C), 121 (L), 125, 133, 134, 135, 148 (B), 155 (BR), 156 (T), 158 (B), 161 (T), 165 (T), 173 (B).

The publishers acknowledge with thanks the cooperation of the following:

RKO; Mercury Productions; Universal; Twentieth Century Fox; Columbia; Edward Small; London Films; British Lion; Rosa Films; CLM–Cocinex; Republic; Lux; Copernic/ Cosmos; Arco/Cineriz/Lyre Film; Transcontinental/Marianne; Woodfall; Famous Artists; Paramount; Dino De Laurentiis/Mosfilm; BBS; Films La Boetie; Warner Brothers; Zenith; ITC; Rank; EMI; MGM; Analysis; CCC; Europa/Hisa; ORTF/Albina.

The publishers would like to thank Carol Schickel for her invaluable research.